Wisdom and Art of Forgiveness

ISBN-10: 1534966323
ISBN-13: 978-1534966321

Acknowledgments

I would like to acknowledge and honor the following people for granting me permission to contribute their quotes of forgiveness in this book:

Doe Zantamata. Jeanne Jones, Jennifer O'Neill, Lori Rubenstein, Marianne Williamson, Naomi Drew, and Neale Donald Walsch.

I would like to acknowledge and honor the following people who are now deceased and continue to be an inspiration for myself and others through their quotes of forgiveness:

Abraham Lincoln, George Herbert, Jesus Christ, Mark Twain, William Shakespeare, Leo Tolstoy, Louisa May Alcott, Oscar Wilde, William Penn, Benjamin Franklin, William Blake, Thomas Jefferson, Mishkat al-Masabih, Martin Luther, Lao Tsu, Kuan Yin, Lord Chesterfield, King Solomon, Josh Billings, Edwin Chaplin, Alexander Pope, and Buddha.

I would also like to acknowledge and thank the people who inspired me to create poetry about forgiveness including the 20 children who were killed at Sandy Hook Elementary, a couple murdered in their car parked in a rest stop, a woman forgiving her ex-husband, a nine year old girl showing courage to forgive a friend, and a wise man's vision of peace in the Middle East.

Introduction

Forgiveness is not an easy road. On my way to forgiveness I traveled down many long roads filled with potholes of resentment and anger. Today I have reached a place of peace knowing that forgiveness does not condone the action; instead, it sets me free from the person or persons I felt caused me harm.

I learned through the creation of this coloring book that forgiveness is essential in my every day life. The quotes in this book reflect the essence of my own personal discovery of forgiveness. They are the bricks laying down the foundation of forgiveness upon which I choose to build my house. The sky is now the limit as I share this book with you and others so we can all soar on the wings of forgiveness.

I Love You
Marita

An Offering of Peace

An offering of peace
a gift of love
connecting with the
heavens above
and the earth below
From this place I grow
rising into the sky
I take wings and fly
out of the ashes of
my past
Forgiveness is felt at
last
I am free to serve through
God's will not mine
as I surrender today
to the divine.
I Love You
Marita
7/11/16

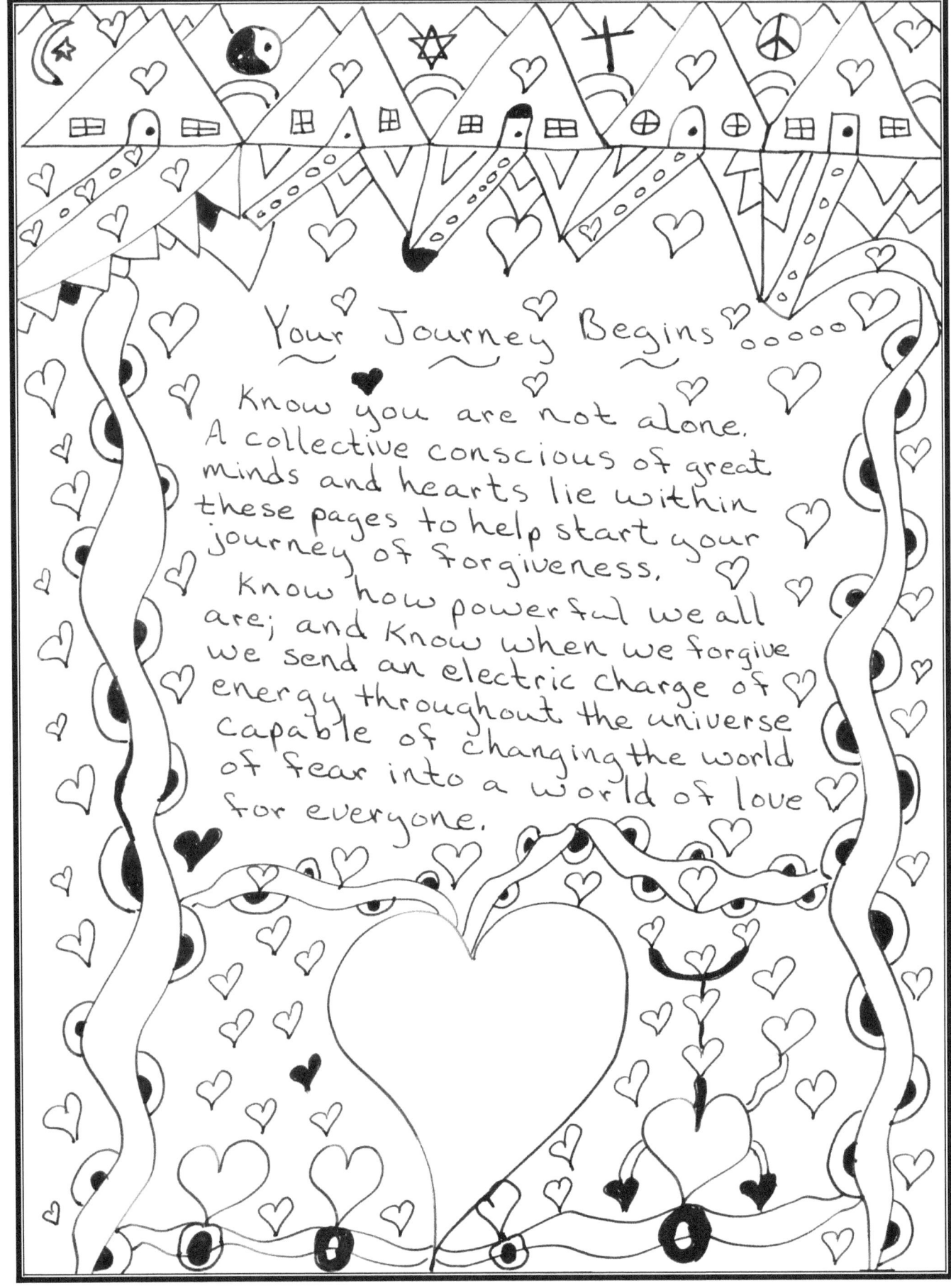

Your Journey Begins

Know you are not alone.
A collective conscious of great
minds and hearts lie within
these pages to help start your
journey of forgiveness.

Know how powerful we all
are; and know when we forgive
we send an electric charge of
energy throughout the universe
capable of changing the world
of fear into a world of love
for everyone.

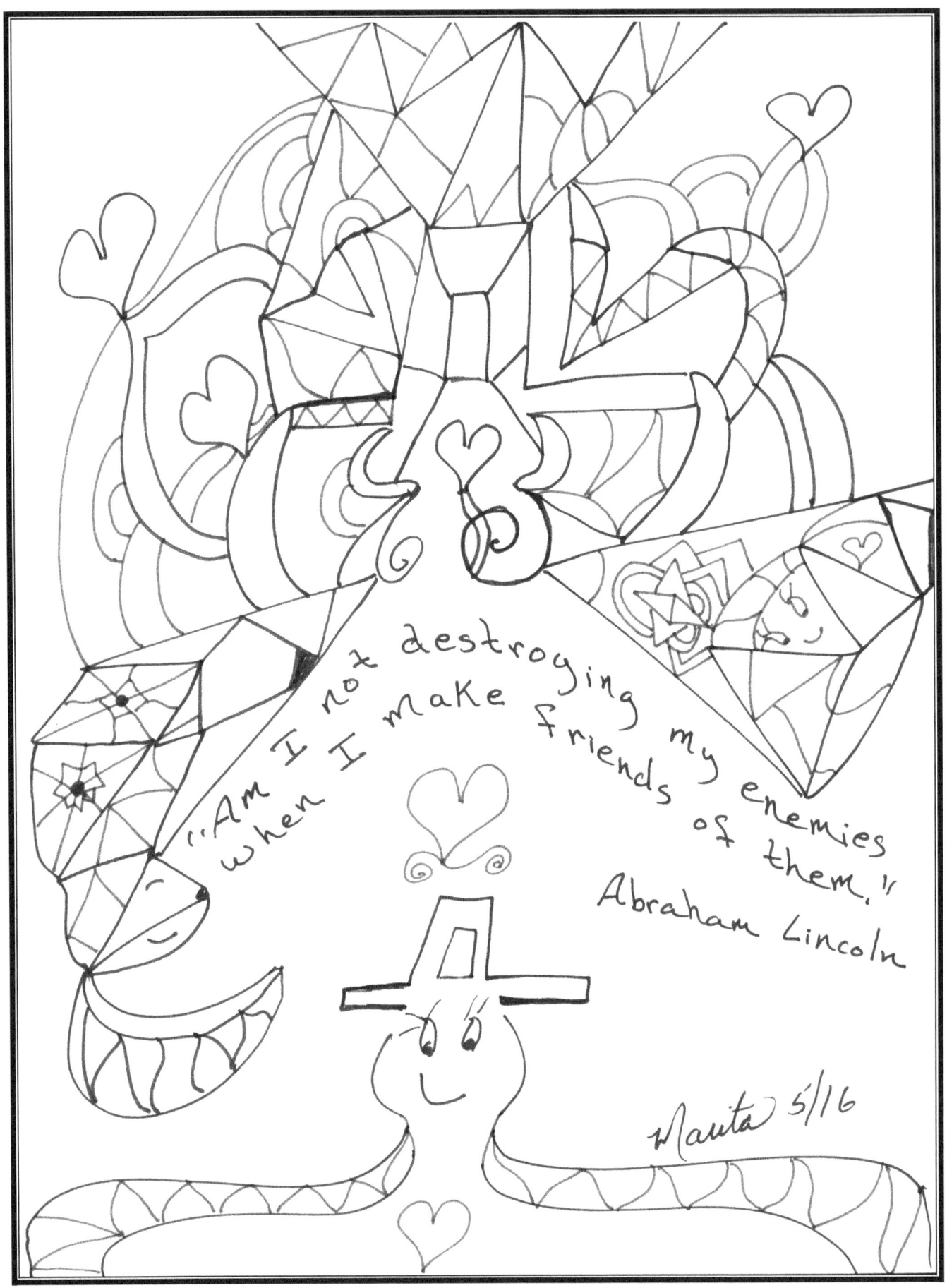

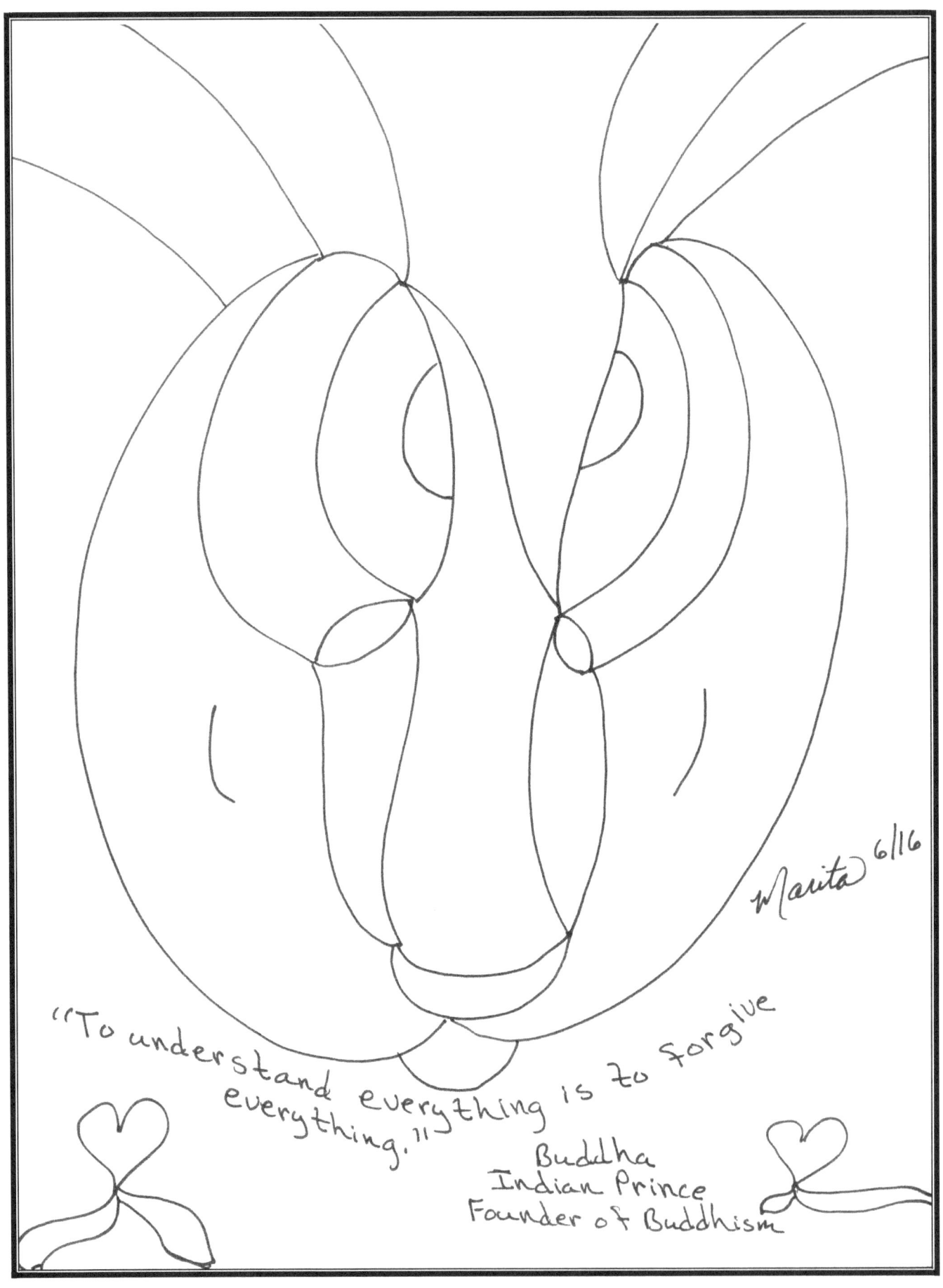

"To understand everything is to forgive everything."

Marita 6/16

Buddha
Indian Prince
Founder of Buddhism

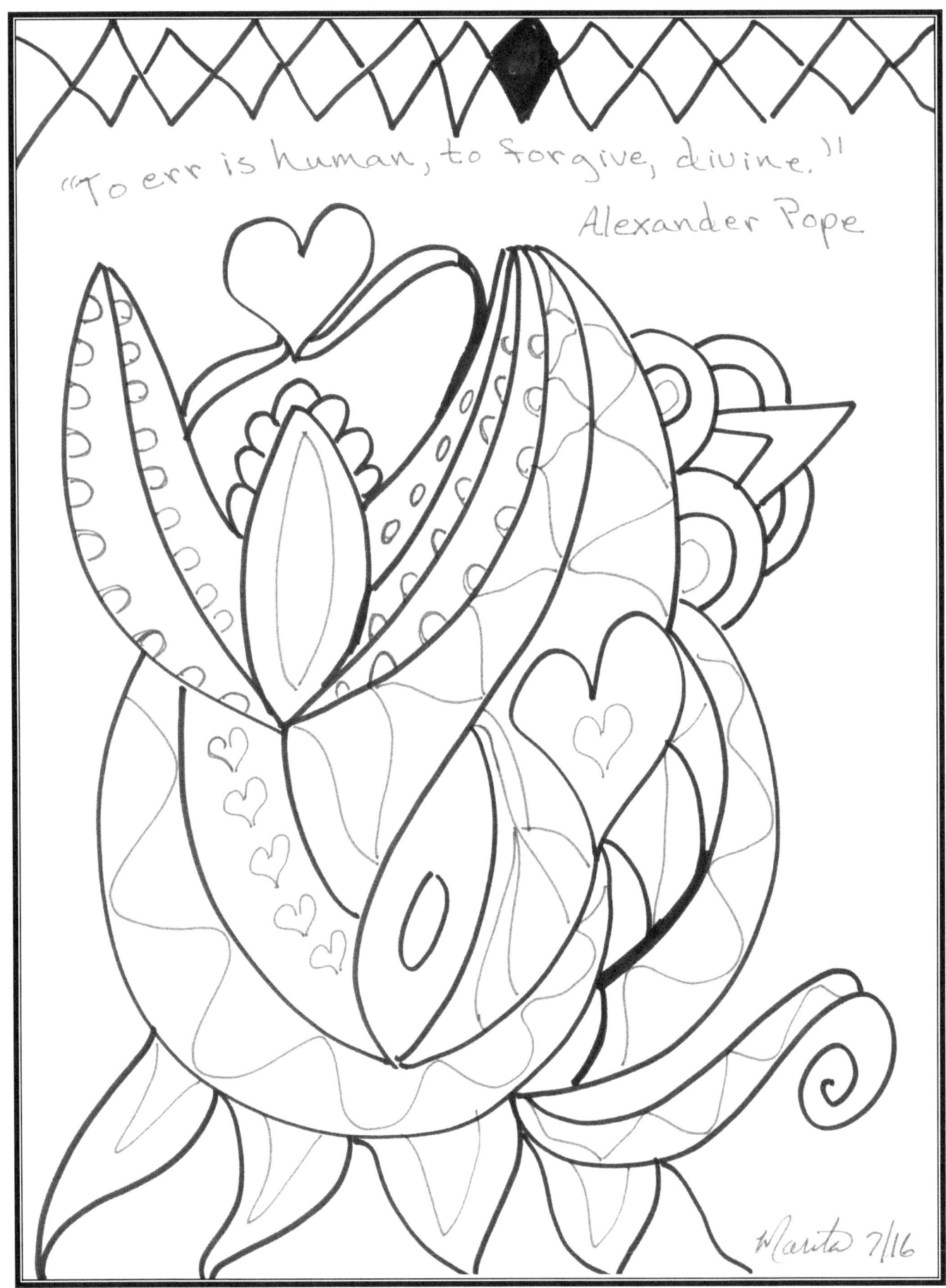

"To err is human, to forgive, divine."

Alexander Pope

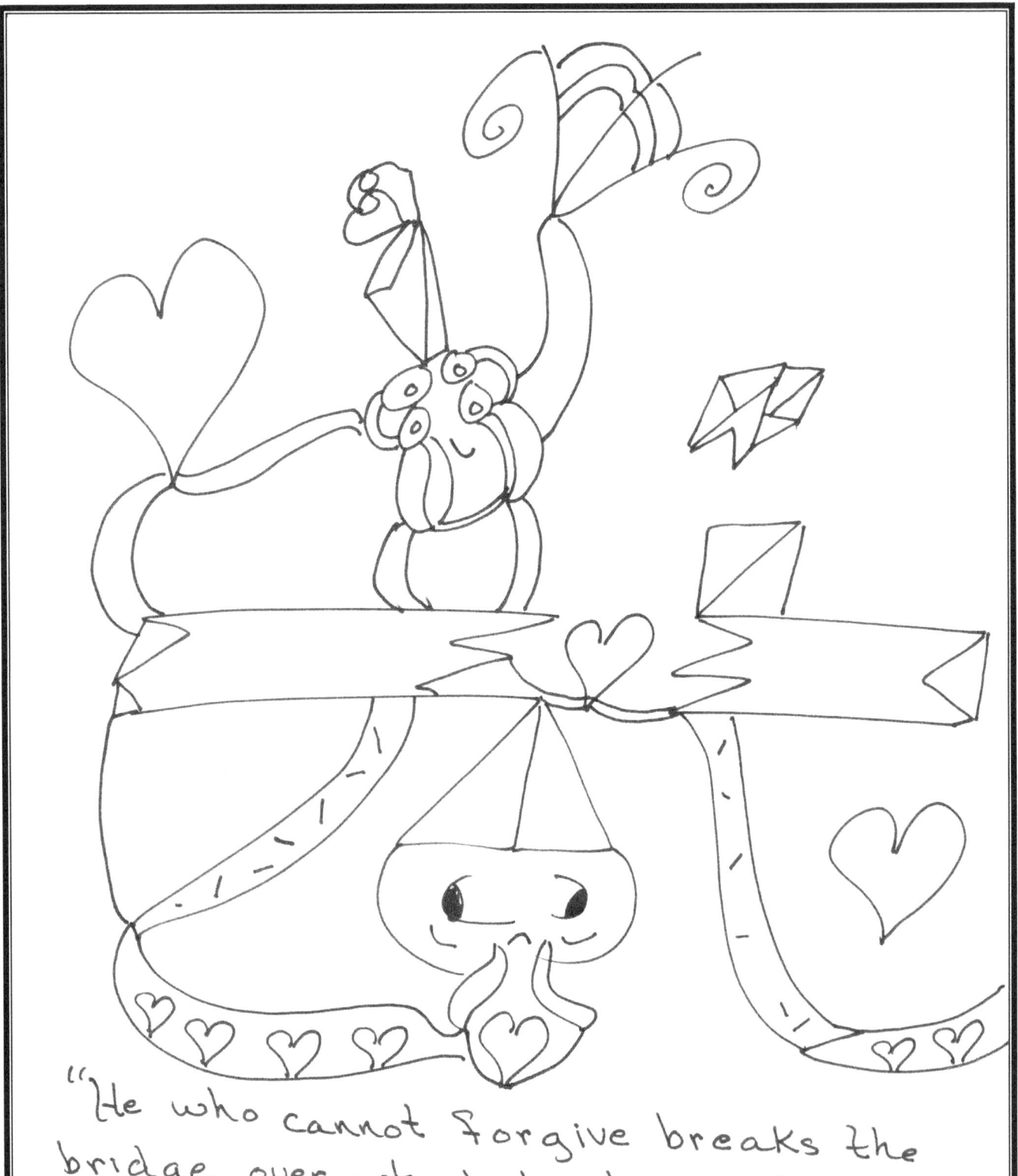

"He who cannot forgive breaks the bridge over which he himself must pass." - George Herbert

Maita 5/16

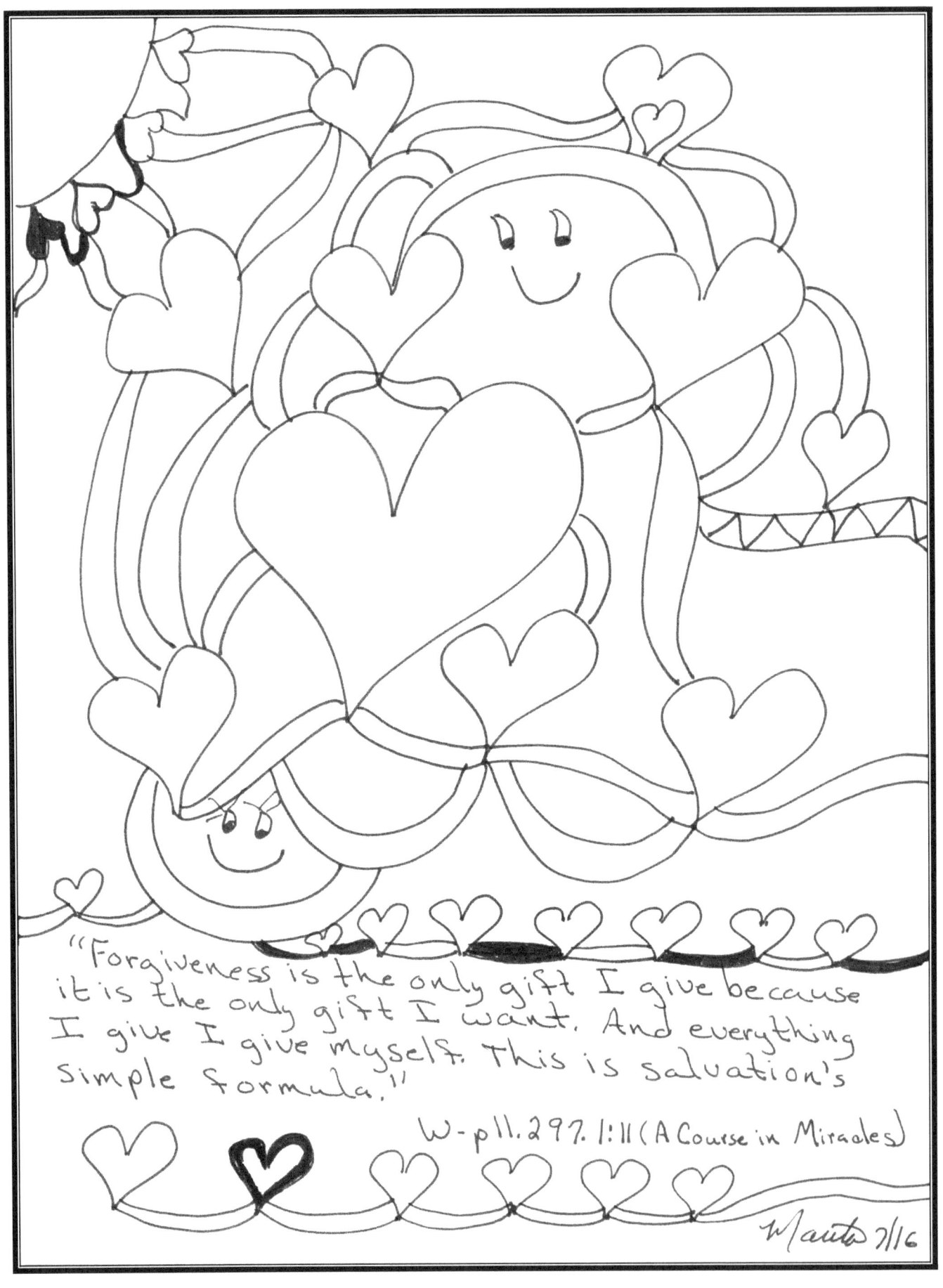

"Forgiveness is the only gift I give because it is the only gift I want. And everything I give I give myself. This is salvation's simple formula."

W-pII.297.1:1-1 (A Course in Miracles)

Marita 7/16

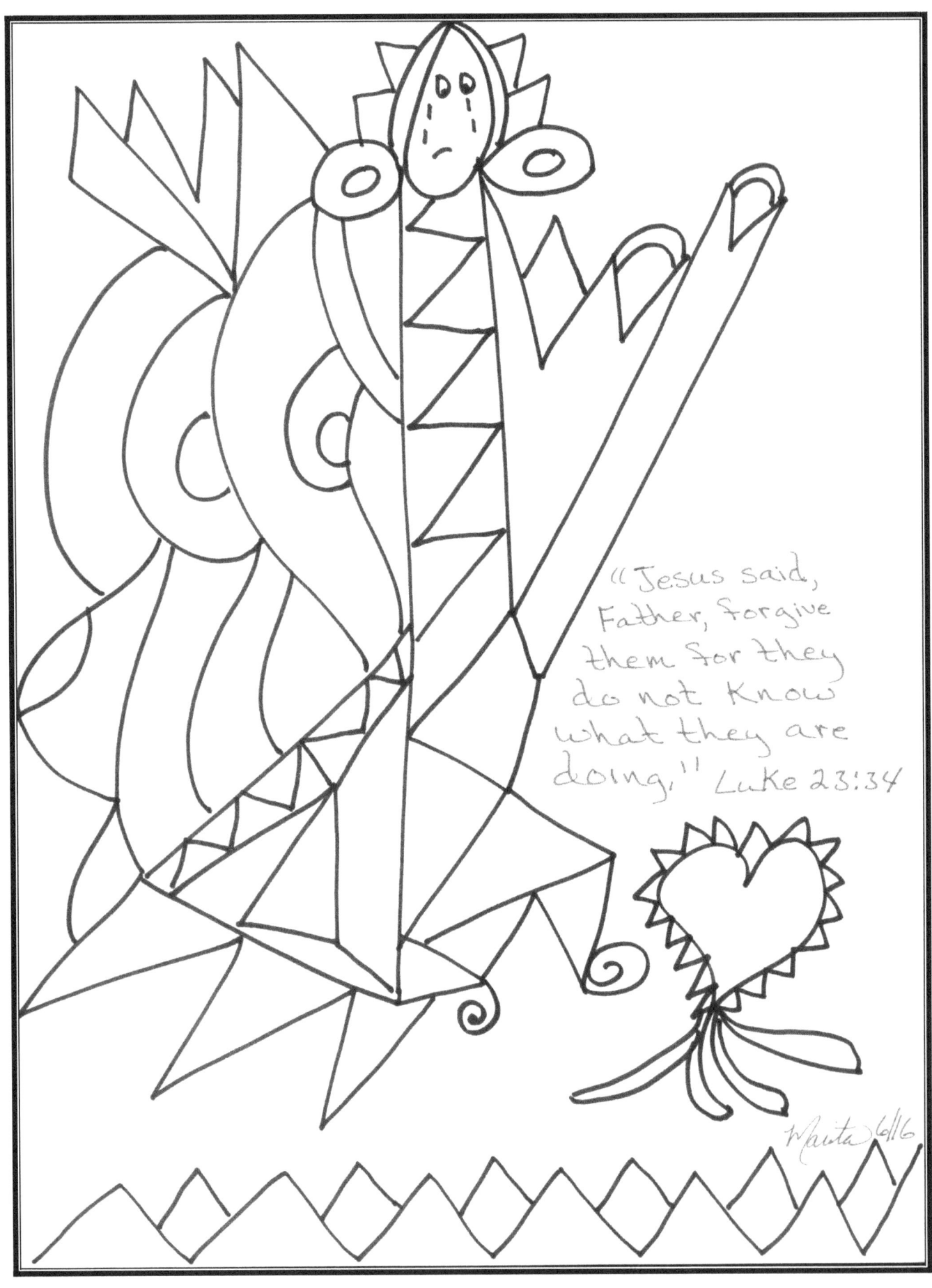

"Jesus said, Father, forgive them for they do not know what they are doing," Luke 23:34

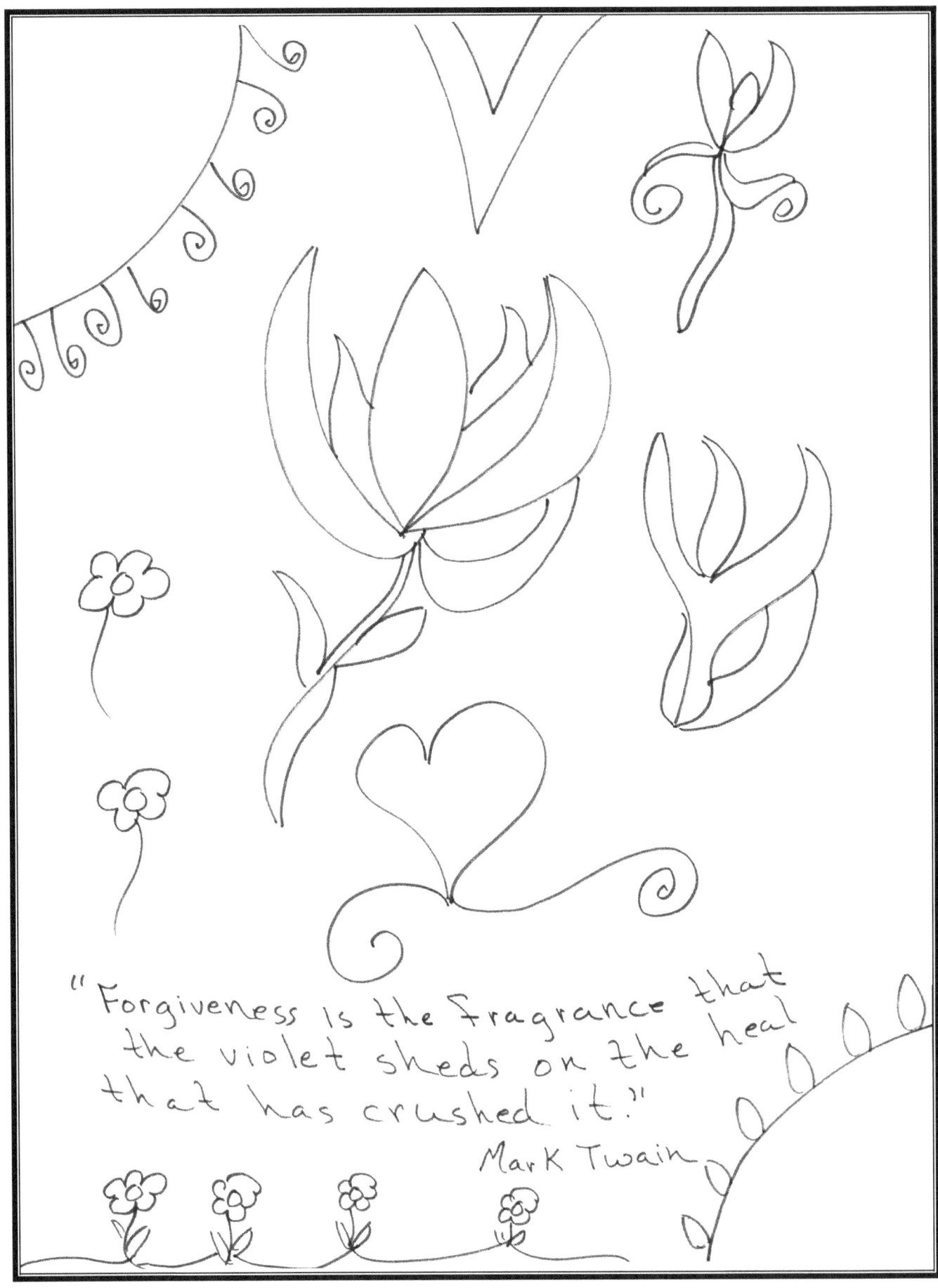

"Forgiveness is the fragrance that the violet sheds on the heal that has crushed it."

Mark Twain

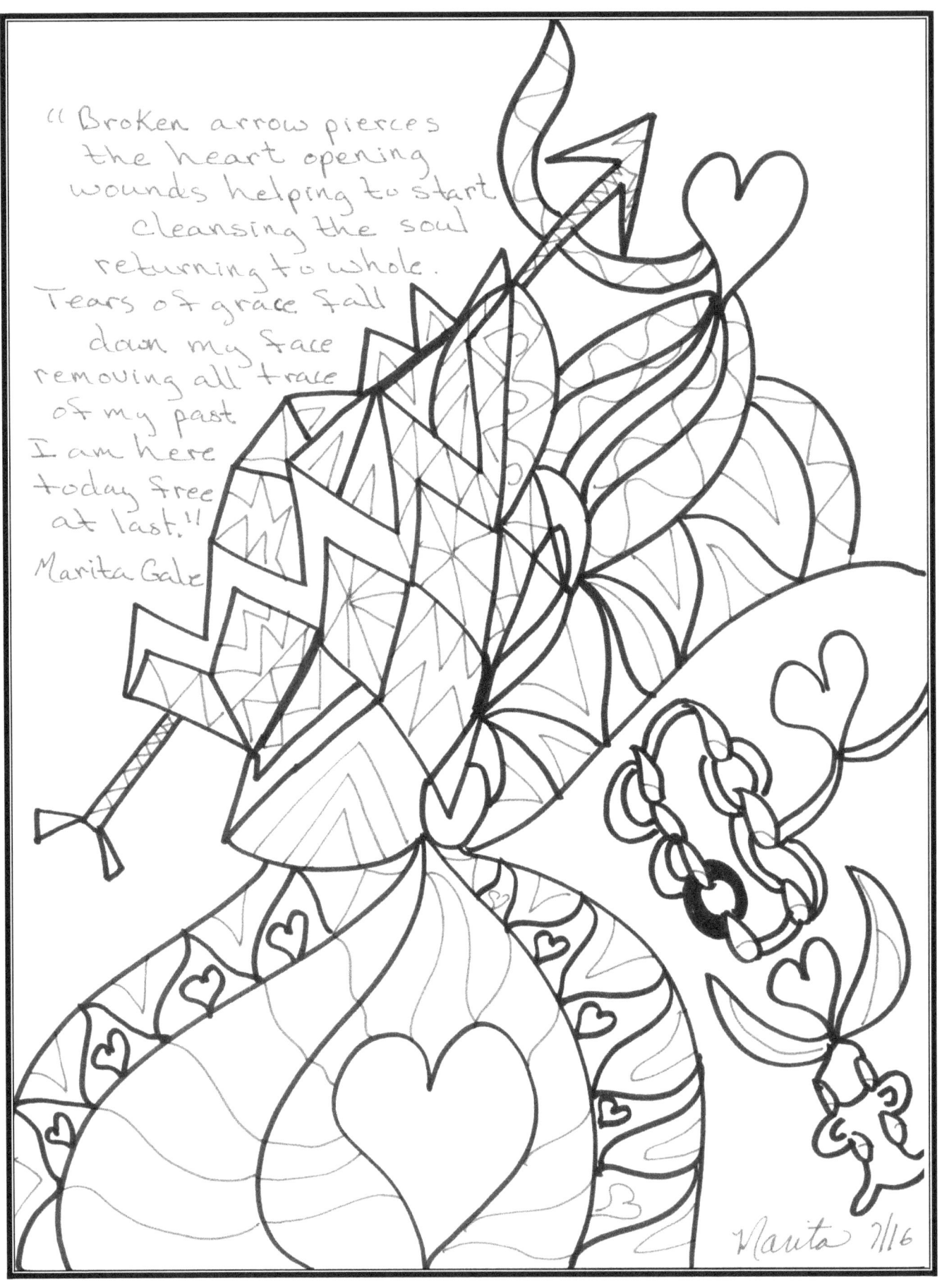

" Broken arrow pierces
the heart opening
wounds helping to start
cleansing the soul
returning to whole.
Tears of grace fall
down my face
removing all trace
of my past
I am here
today free
at last.!!

Marita Gale

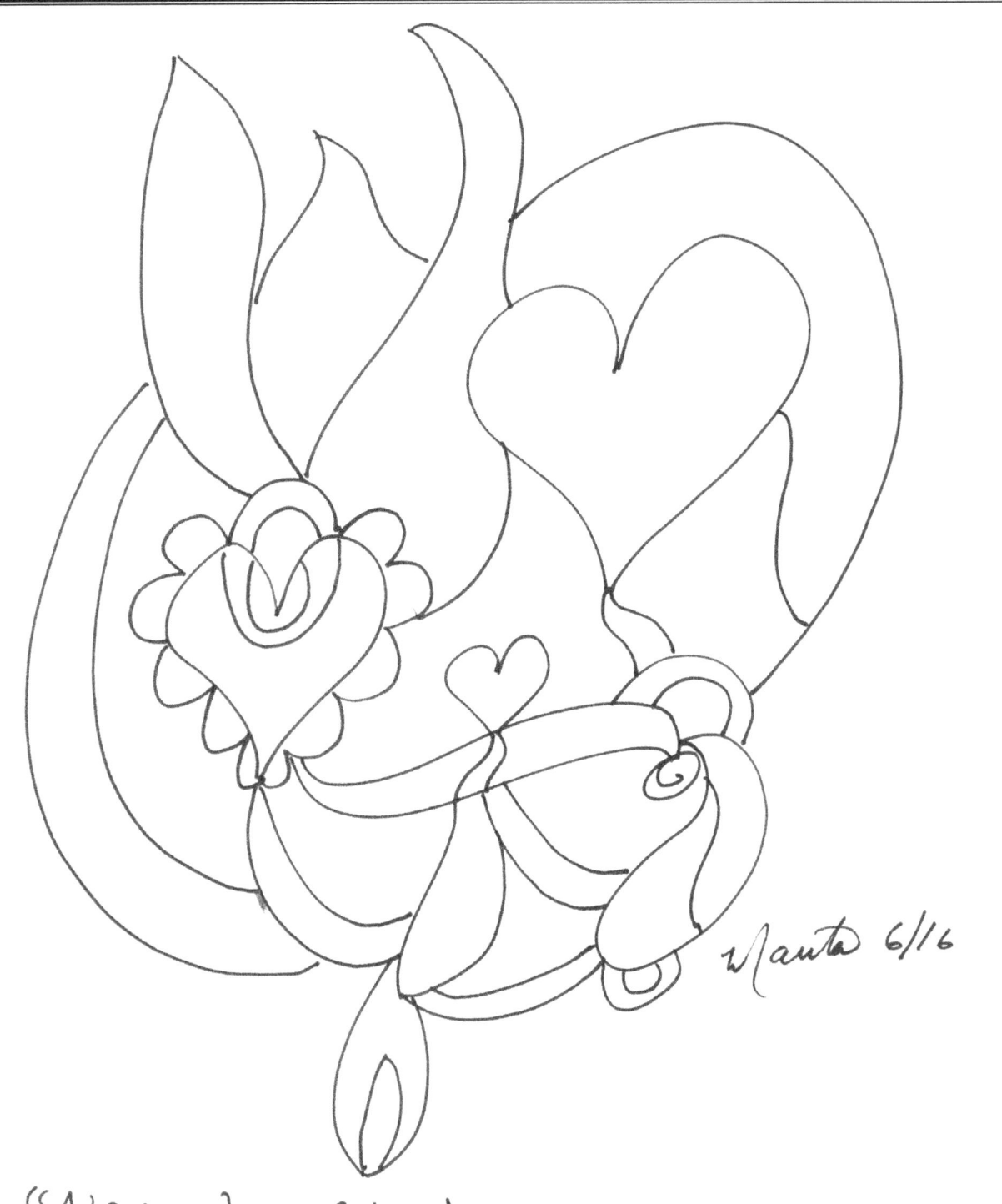

Manta 6/16

"Never does the human soul appear
so strong as when it forgoes revenge
and dares to forgive an injury."
Edwin Hubbel Chaplin

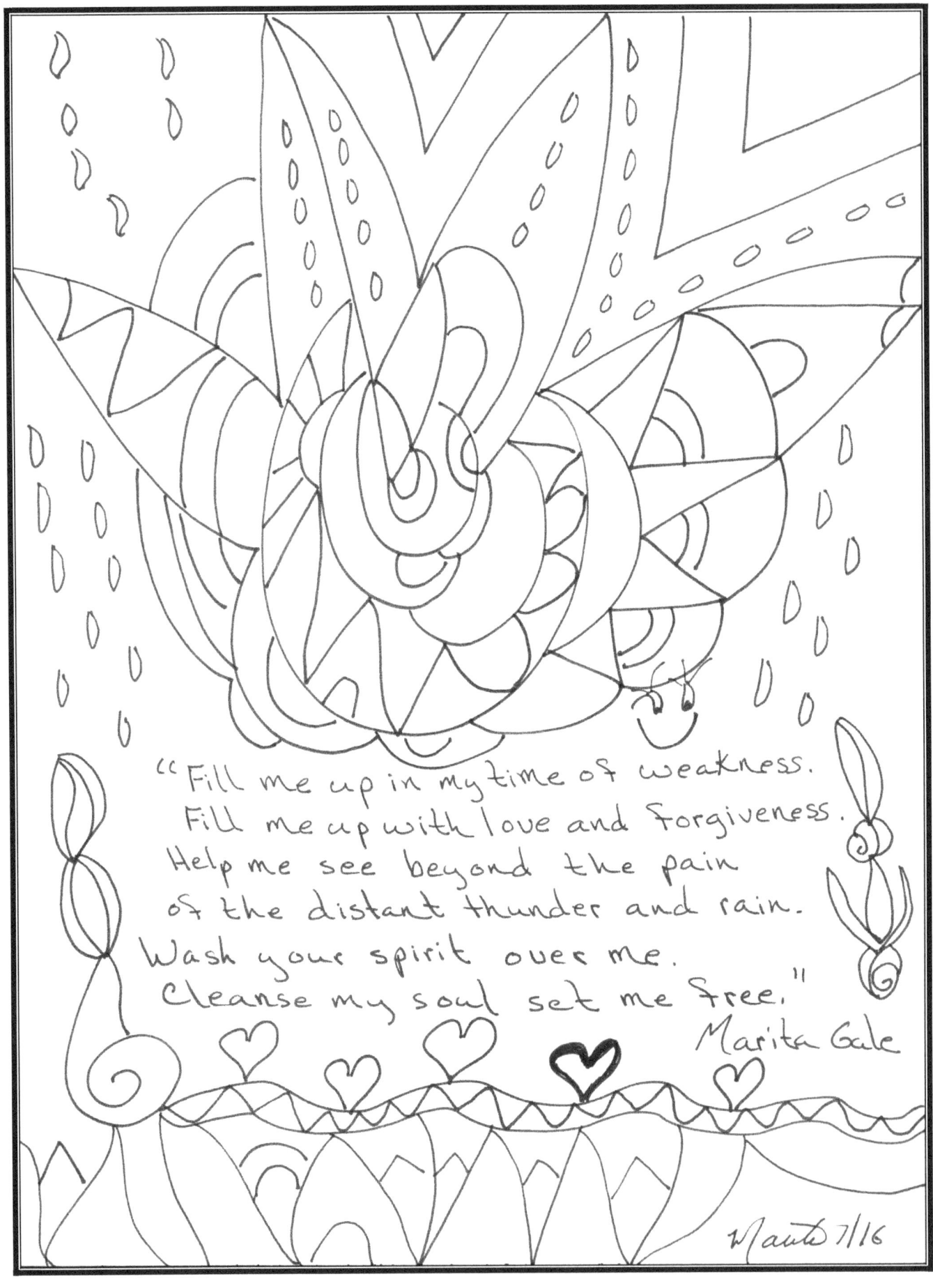

"Fill me up in my time of weakness.
Fill me up with love and forgiveness.
Help me see beyond the pain
of the distant thunder and rain.
Wash your spirit over me.
Cleanse my soul set me free."
Marita Gale

Maarten 7/16

.

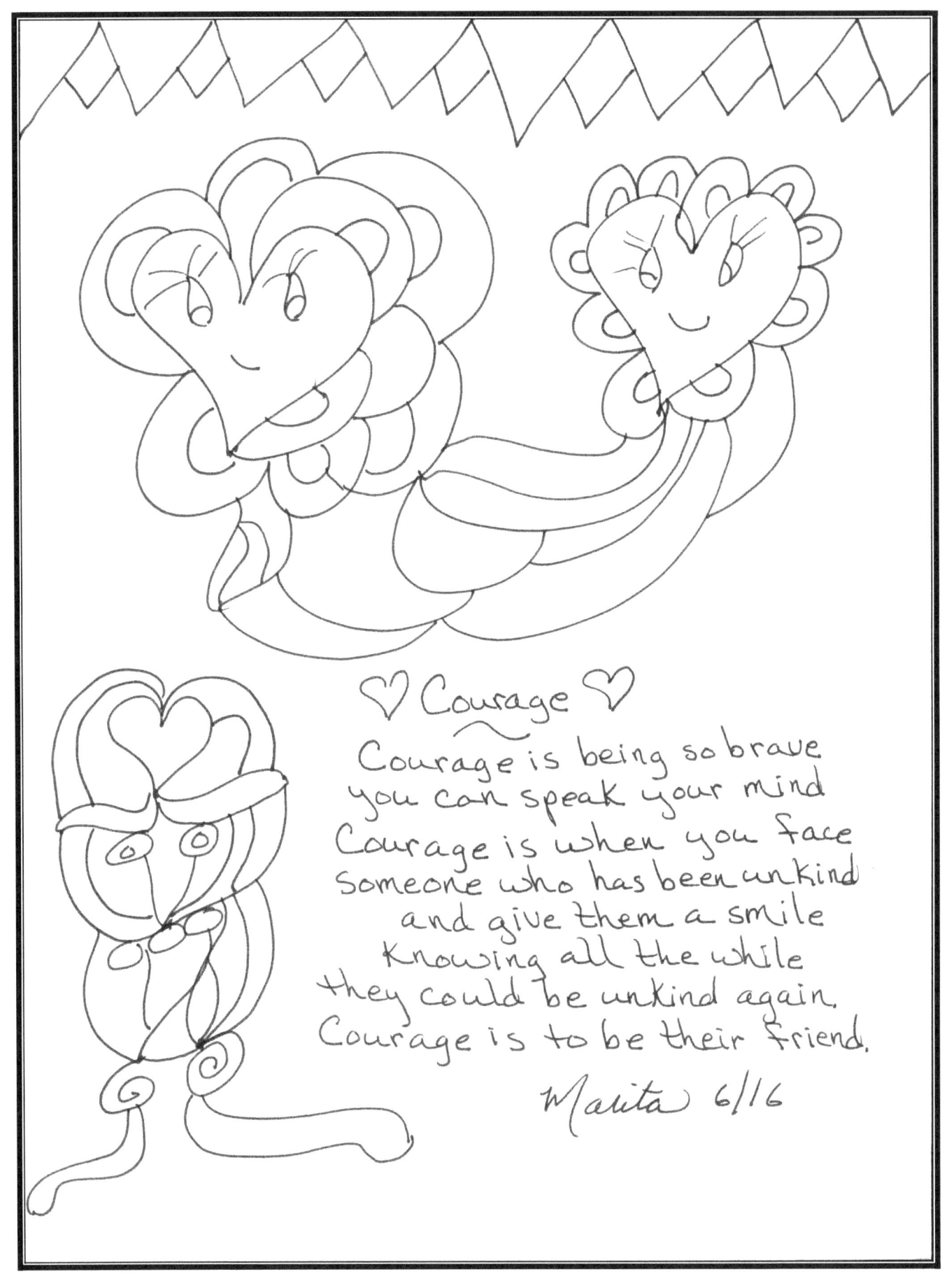

♡ Courage ♡

Courage is being so brave
you can speak your mind
Courage is when you face
someone who has been unkind
and give them a smile
knowing all the while
they could be unkind again.
Courage is to be their friend.

Marita 6/16

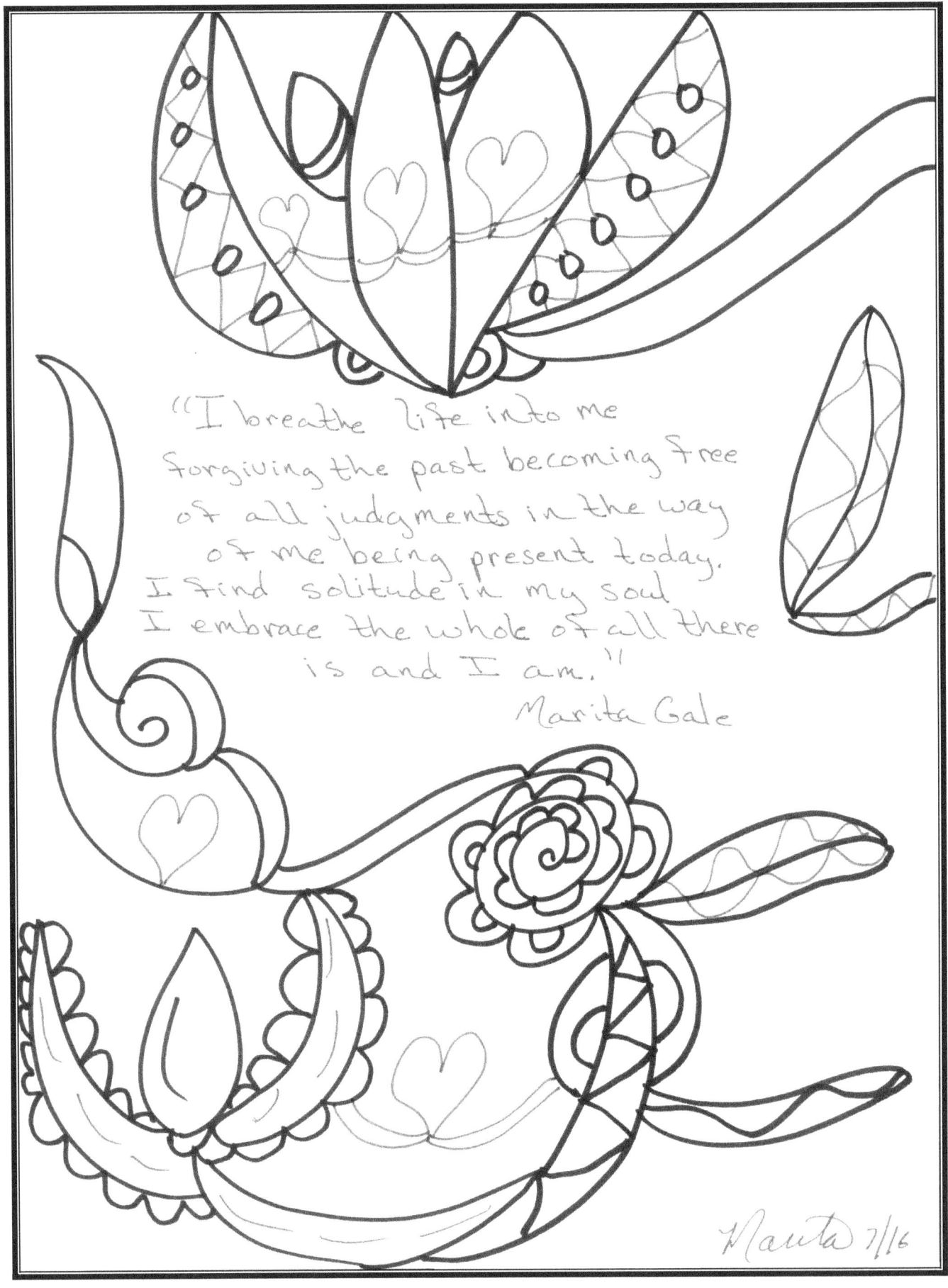

"I breathe life into me
forgiving the past becoming free
of all judgments in the way
of me being present today.
I find solitude in my soul
I embrace the whole of all there
is and I am."
Marita Gale

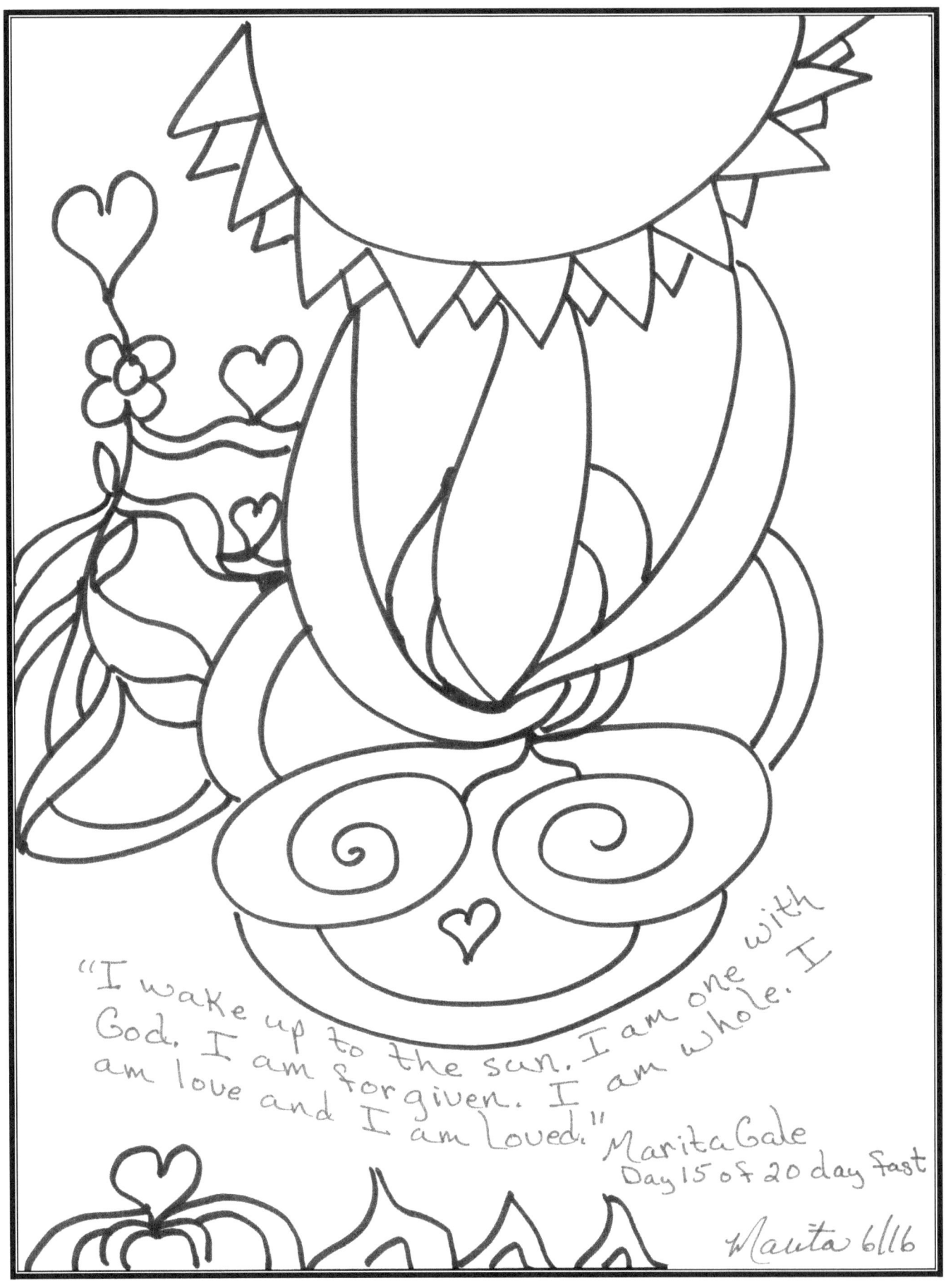

"I wake up to the sun. I am one with God. I am forgiven. I am whole. I am love and I am Loved." Marita Gale
Day 15 of 20 day fast

Marita 6/16

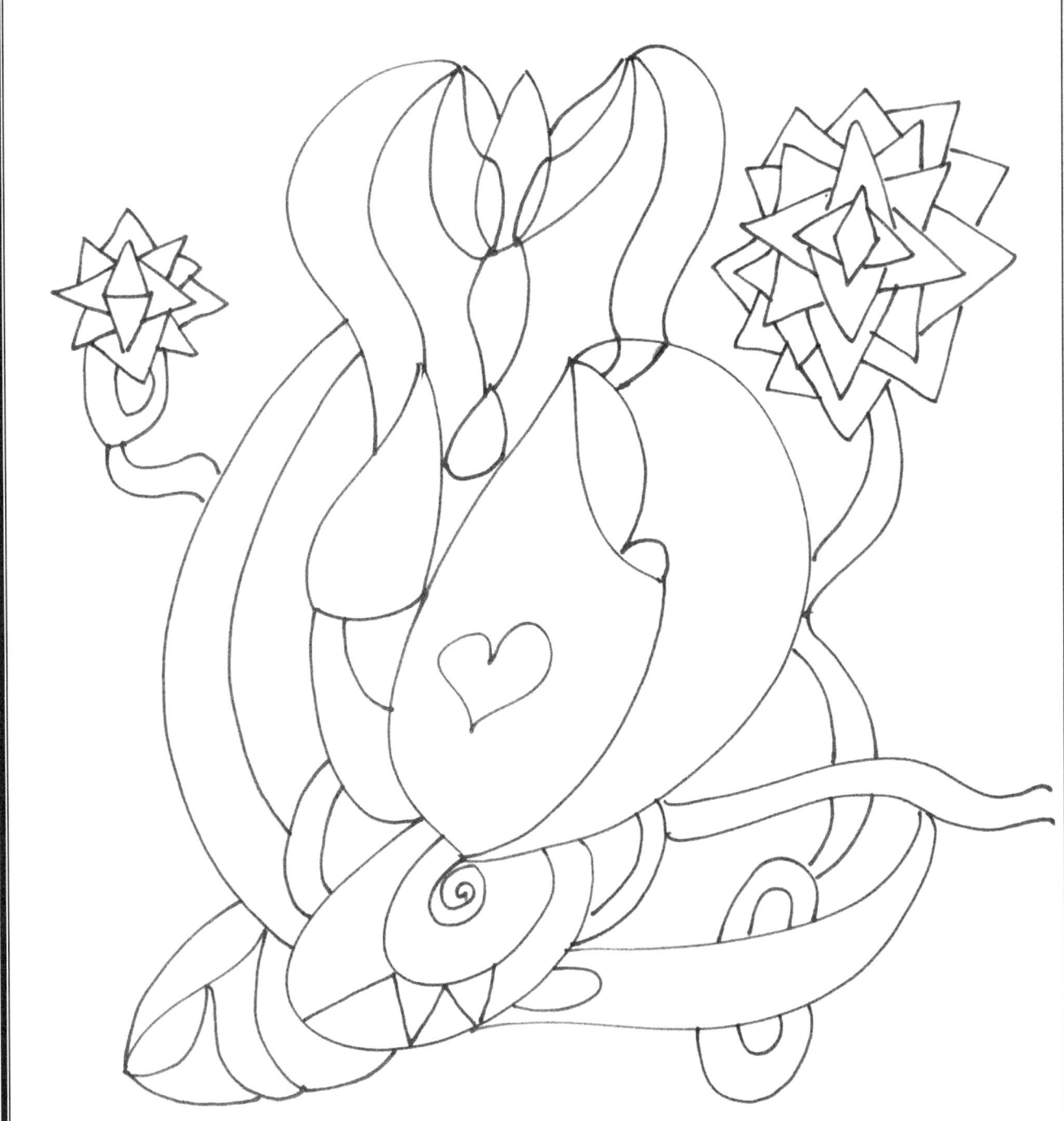

"Their sins and lawless acts I will remember no more."

Hebrews 10:17

Manta 6/16

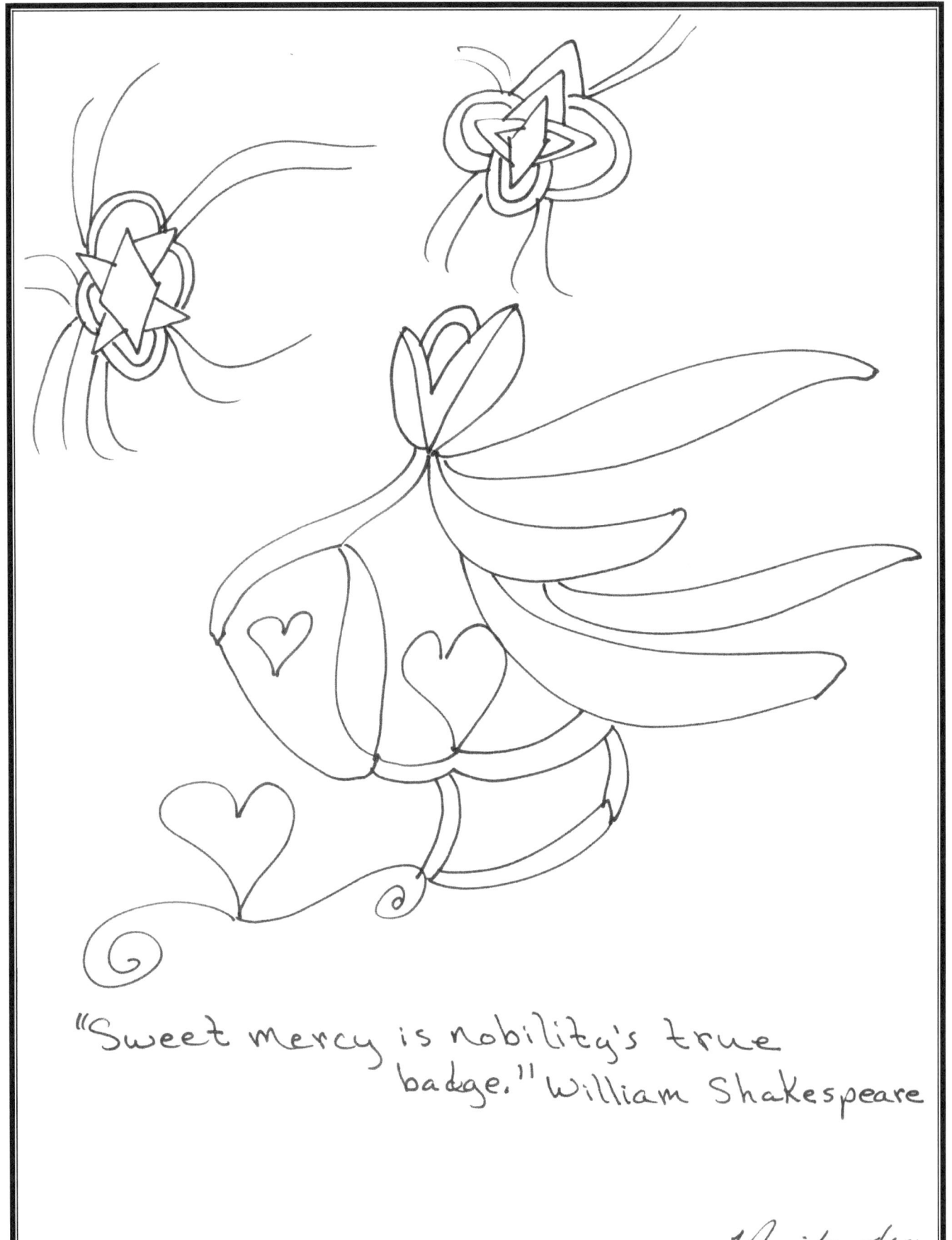

"Sweet mercy is nobility's true badge." William Shakespeare

Maita 5/16

"I do not harbour grudges at all,
I rage for a minute and then forget
about it."
                    Jeanne Jones

Marita 6/16

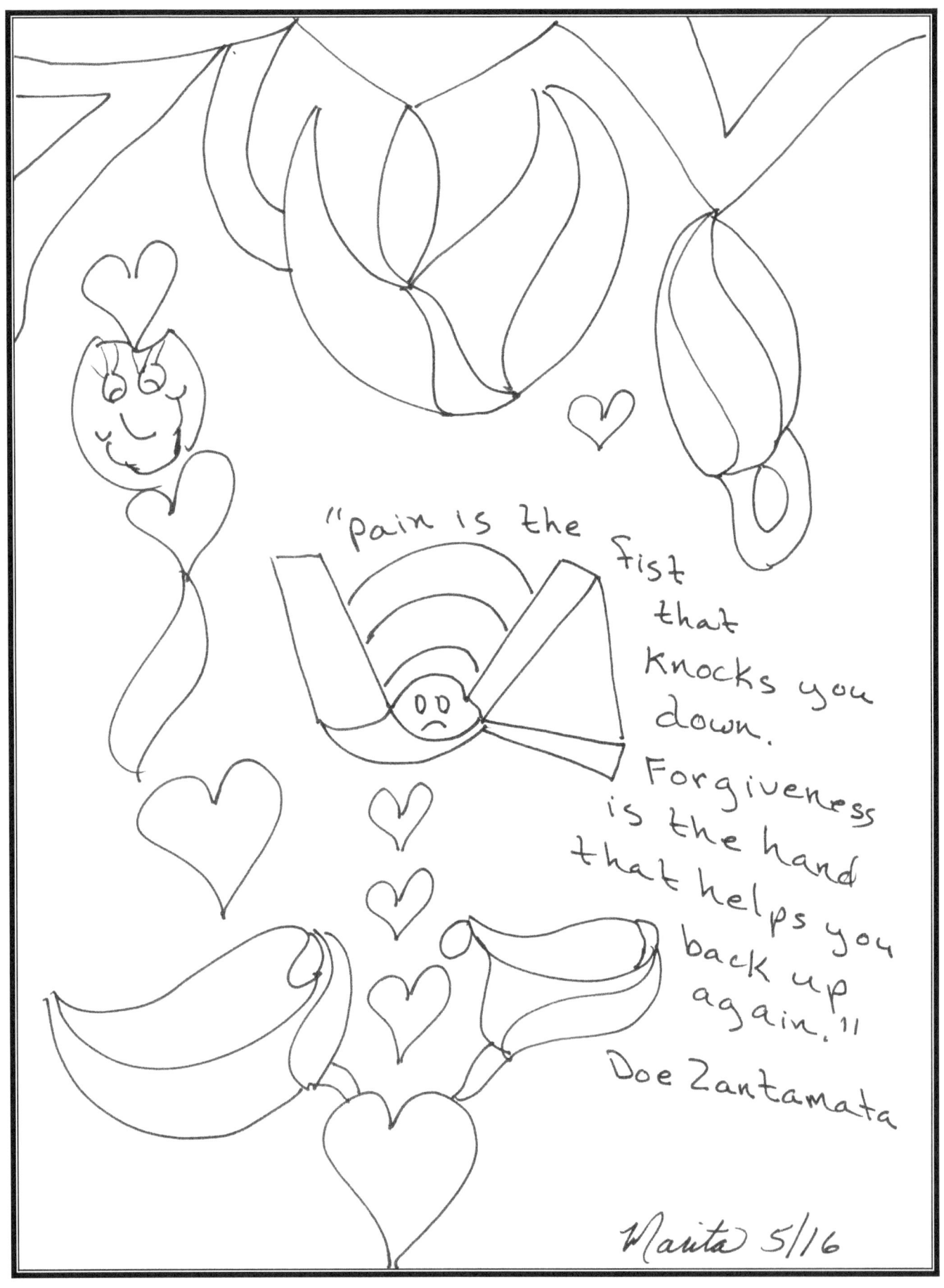

"pain is the fist that knocks you down. Forgiveness is the hand that helps you back up again."

Doe Zantamata

Marita 5/16

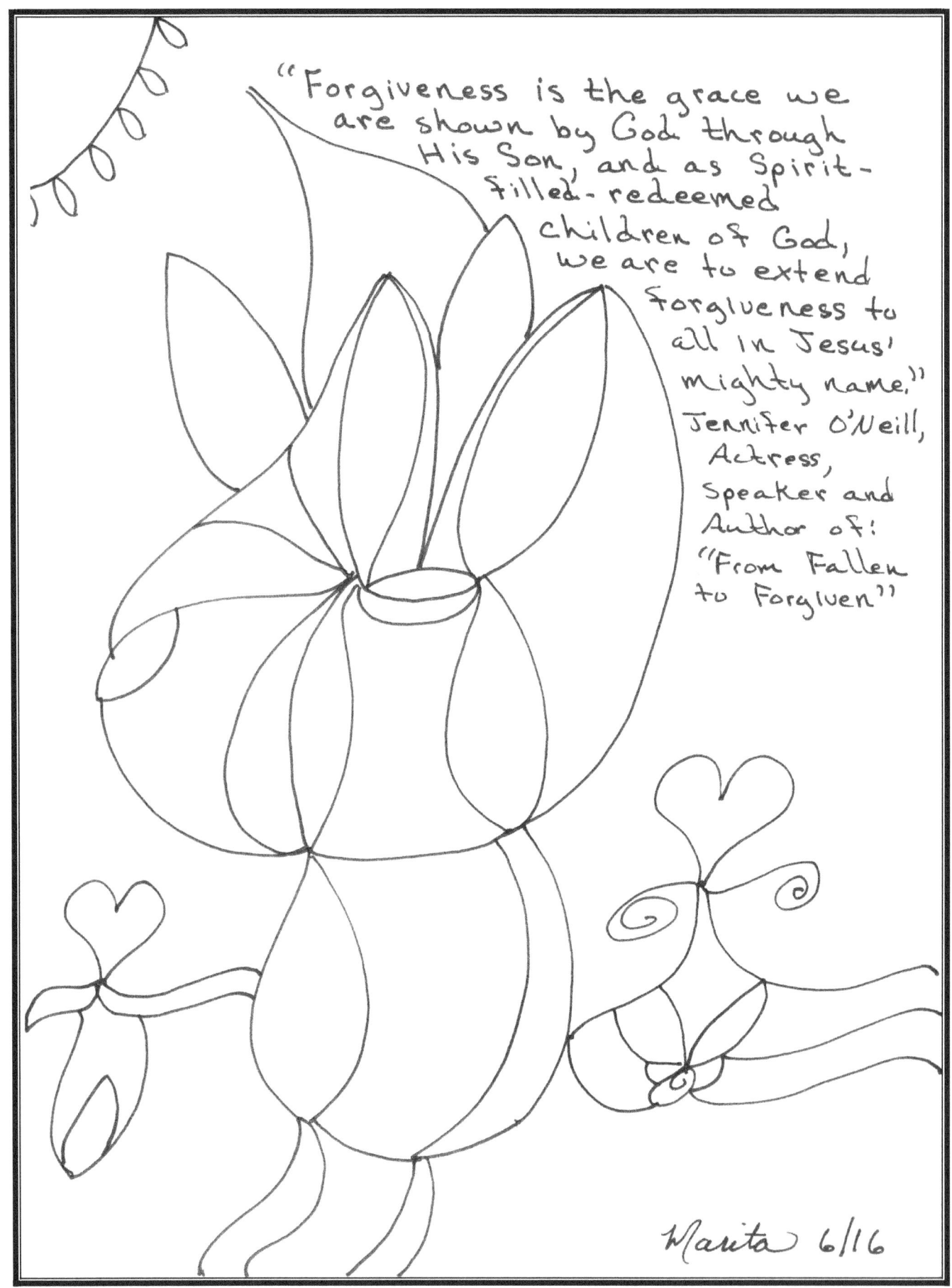

"Forgiveness is the grace we are shown by God through His Son, and as Spirit-filled-redeemed children of God, we are to extend forgiveness to all in Jesus' mighty name."
Jennifer O'Neill,
Actress,
Speaker and
Author of:
"From Fallen to Forgiven"

Marita 6/16

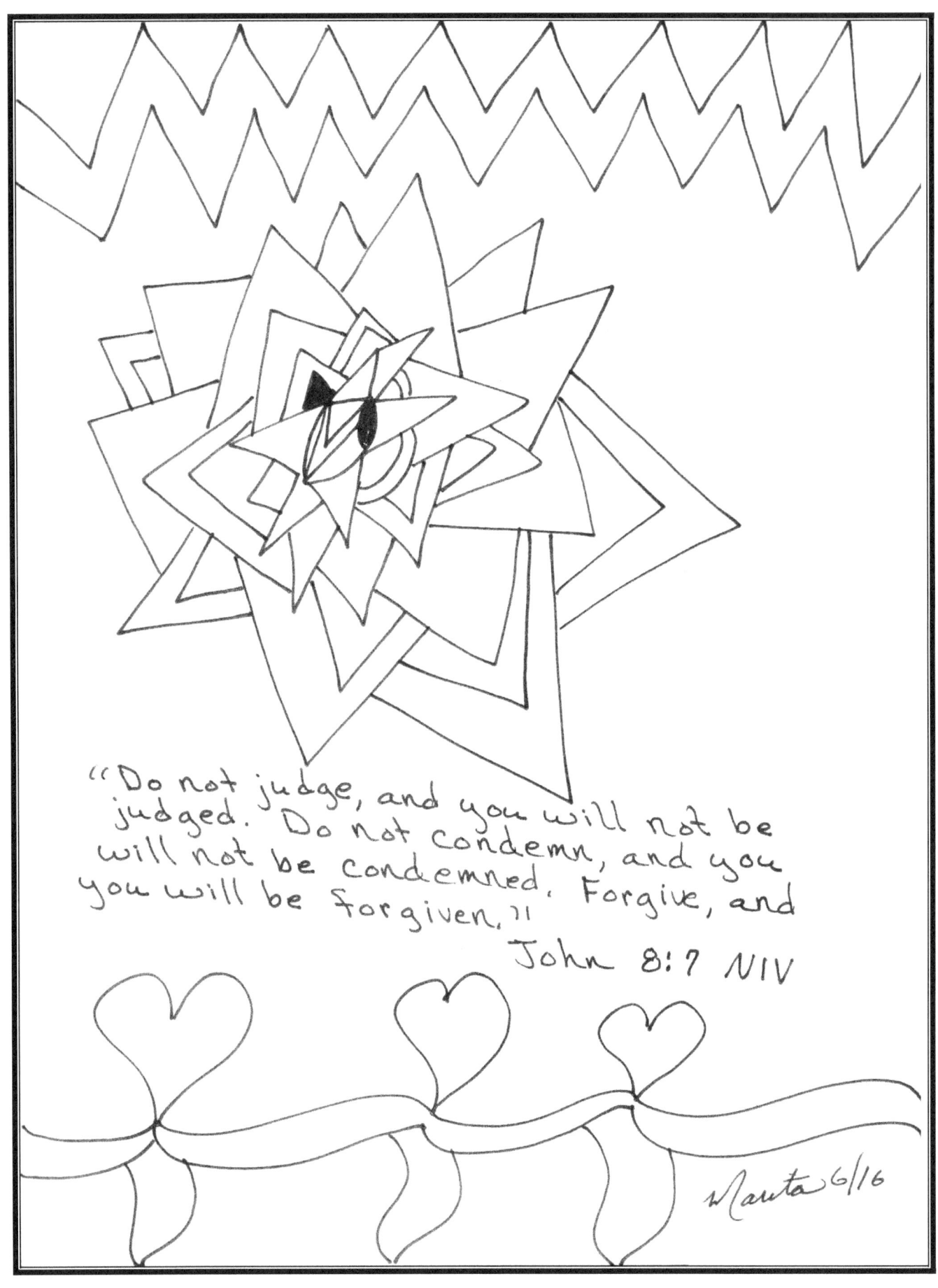

"Do not judge, and you will not be judged. Do not condemn, and you will not be condemned. Forgive, and you will be forgiven."

John 8:7 NIV

Marta 6/16

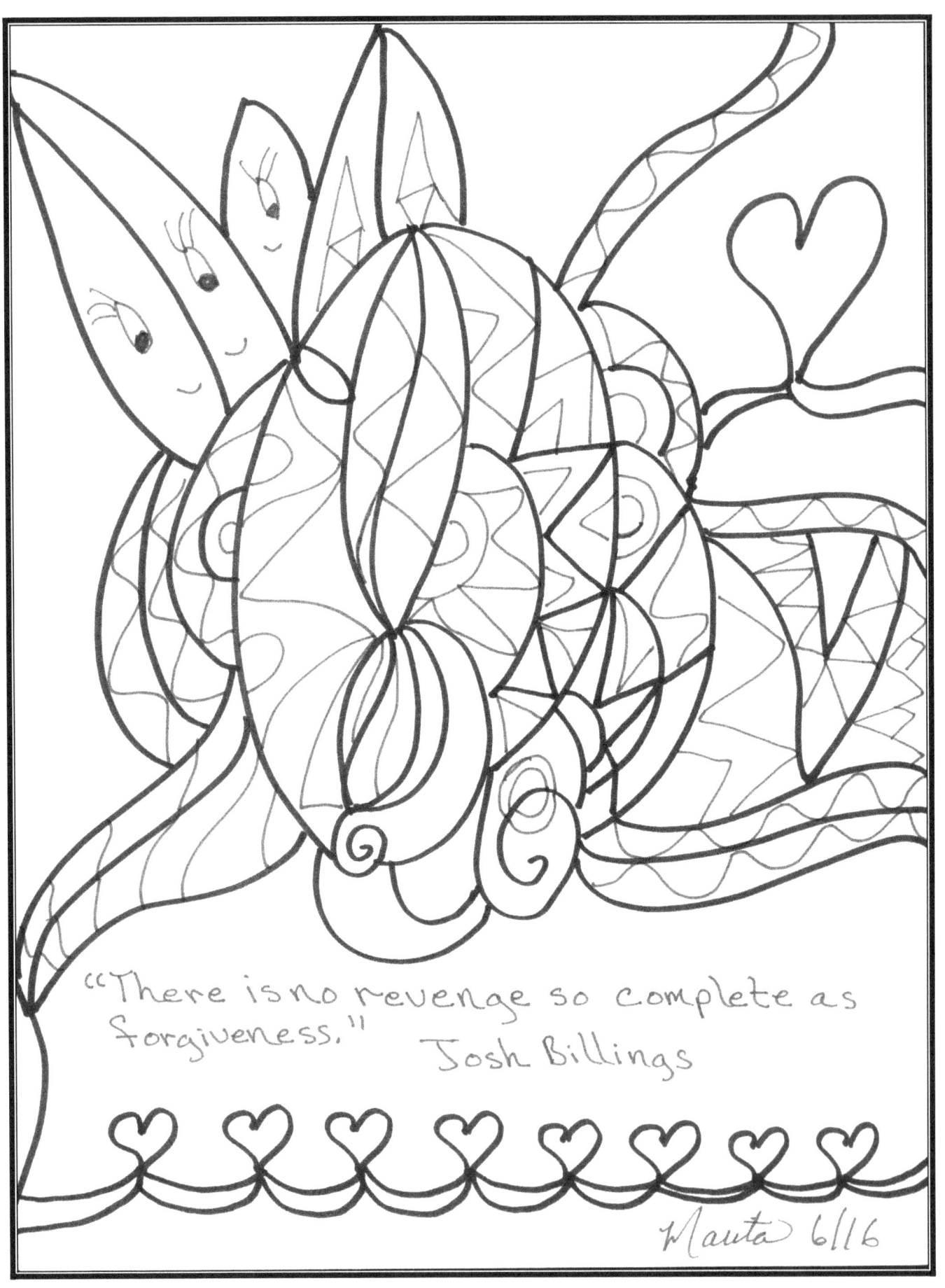

"There is no revenge so complete as forgiveness." Josh Billings

Marta 6/16

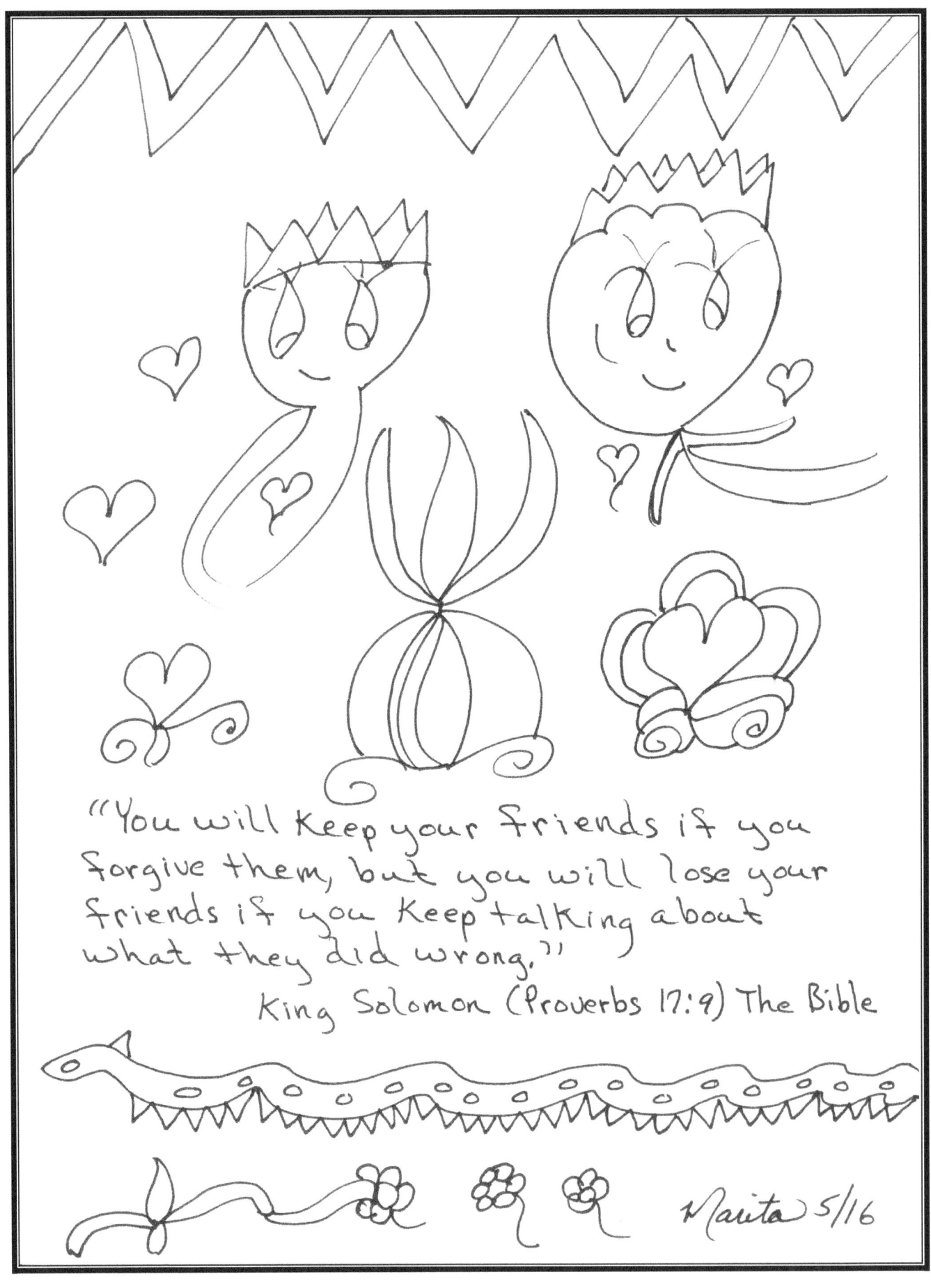

"You will keep your friends if you forgive them, but you will lose your friends if you keep talking about what they did wrong."

King Solomon (Proverbs 17:9) The Bible

Marita 5/16

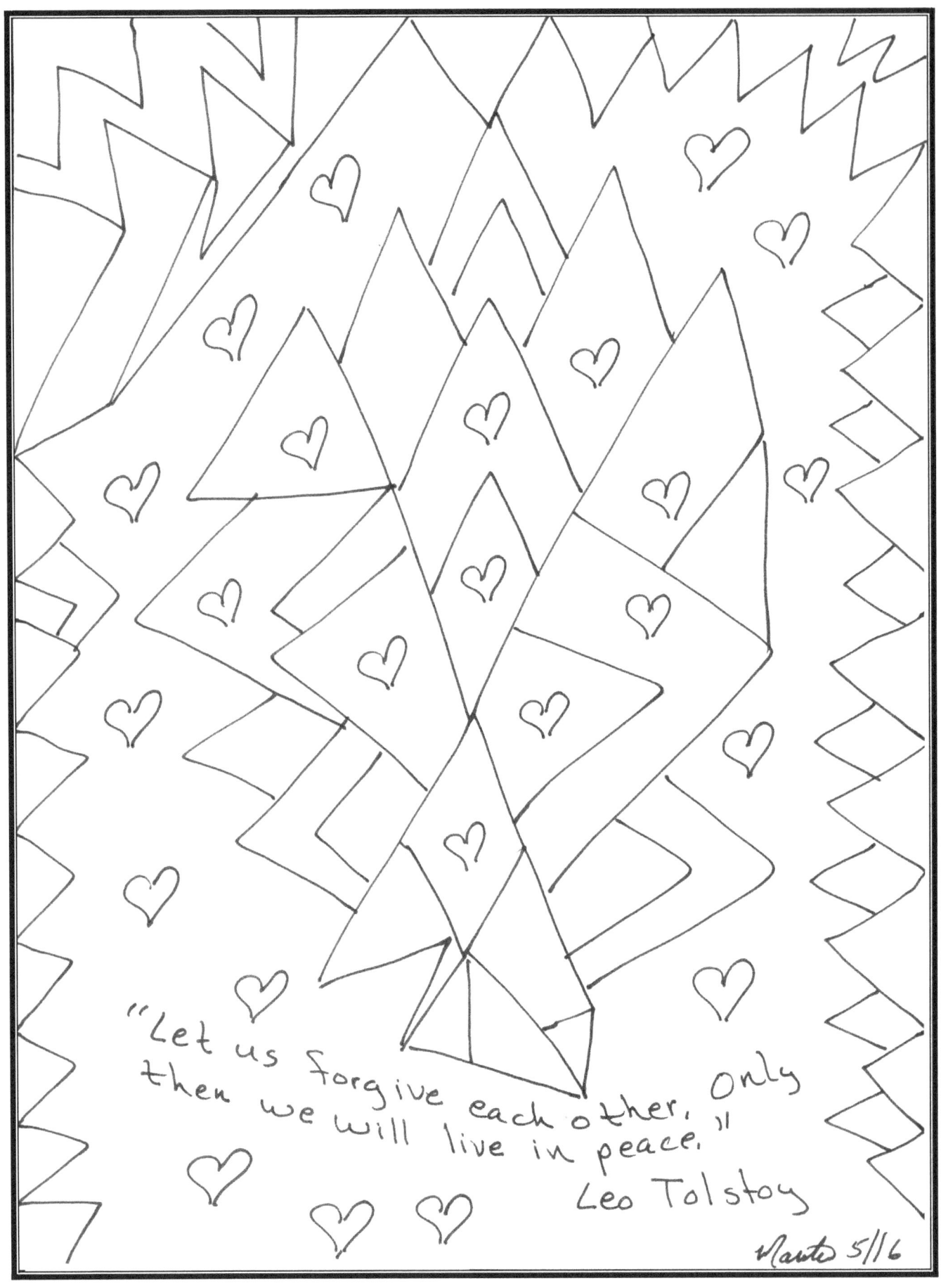

"Let us forgive each other, only then we will live in peace."

Leo Tolstoy

Marto 5/16

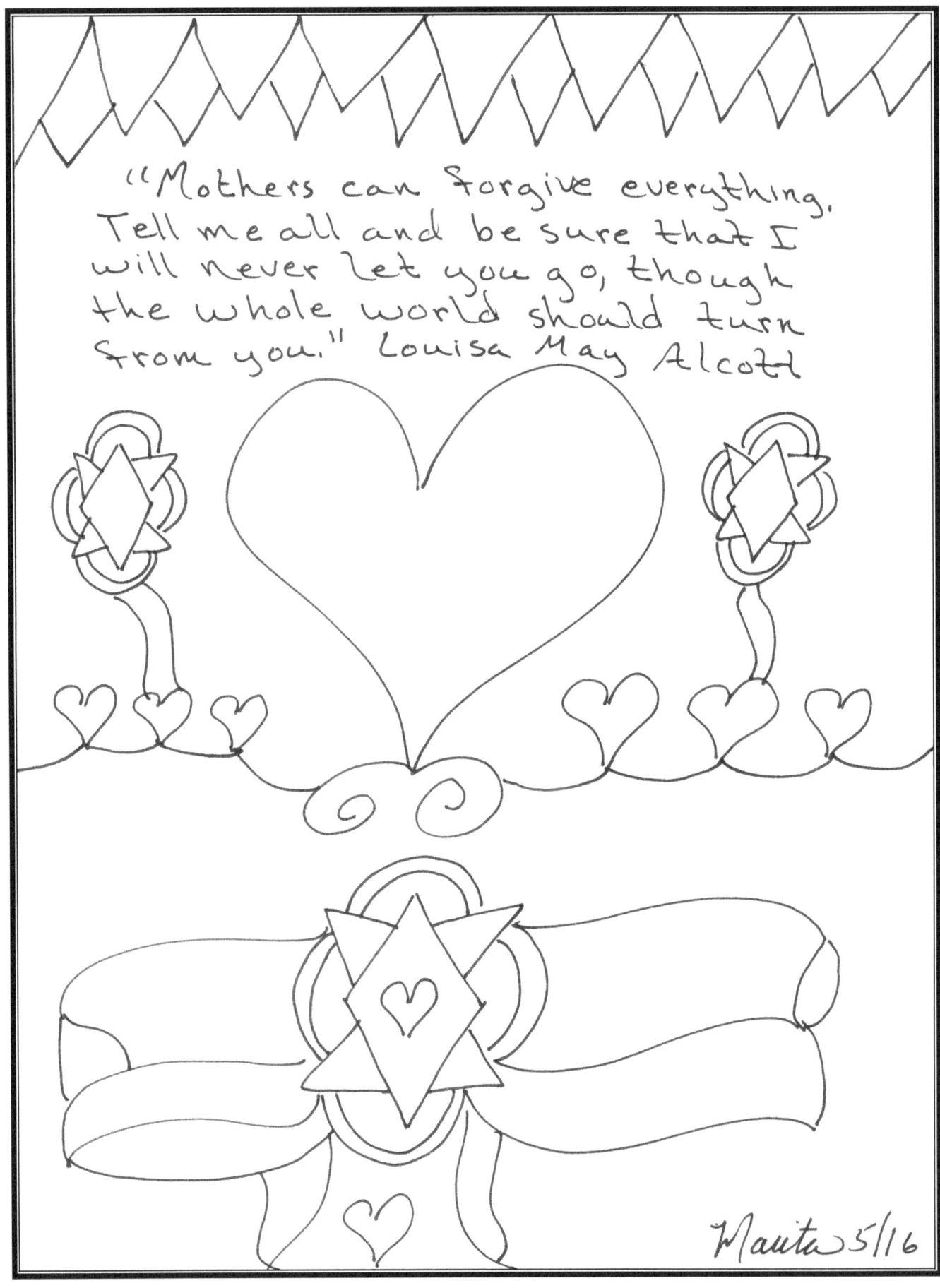

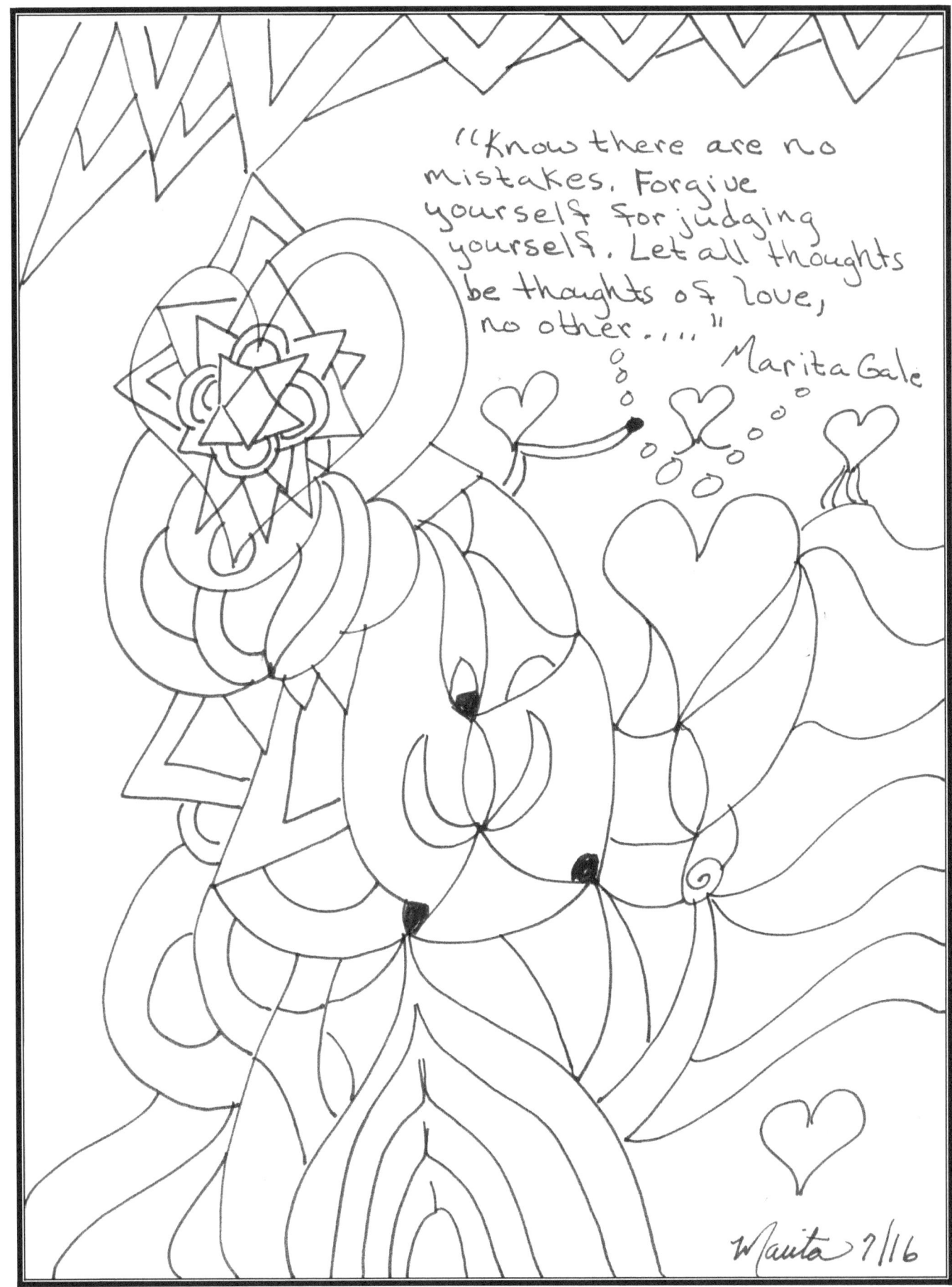

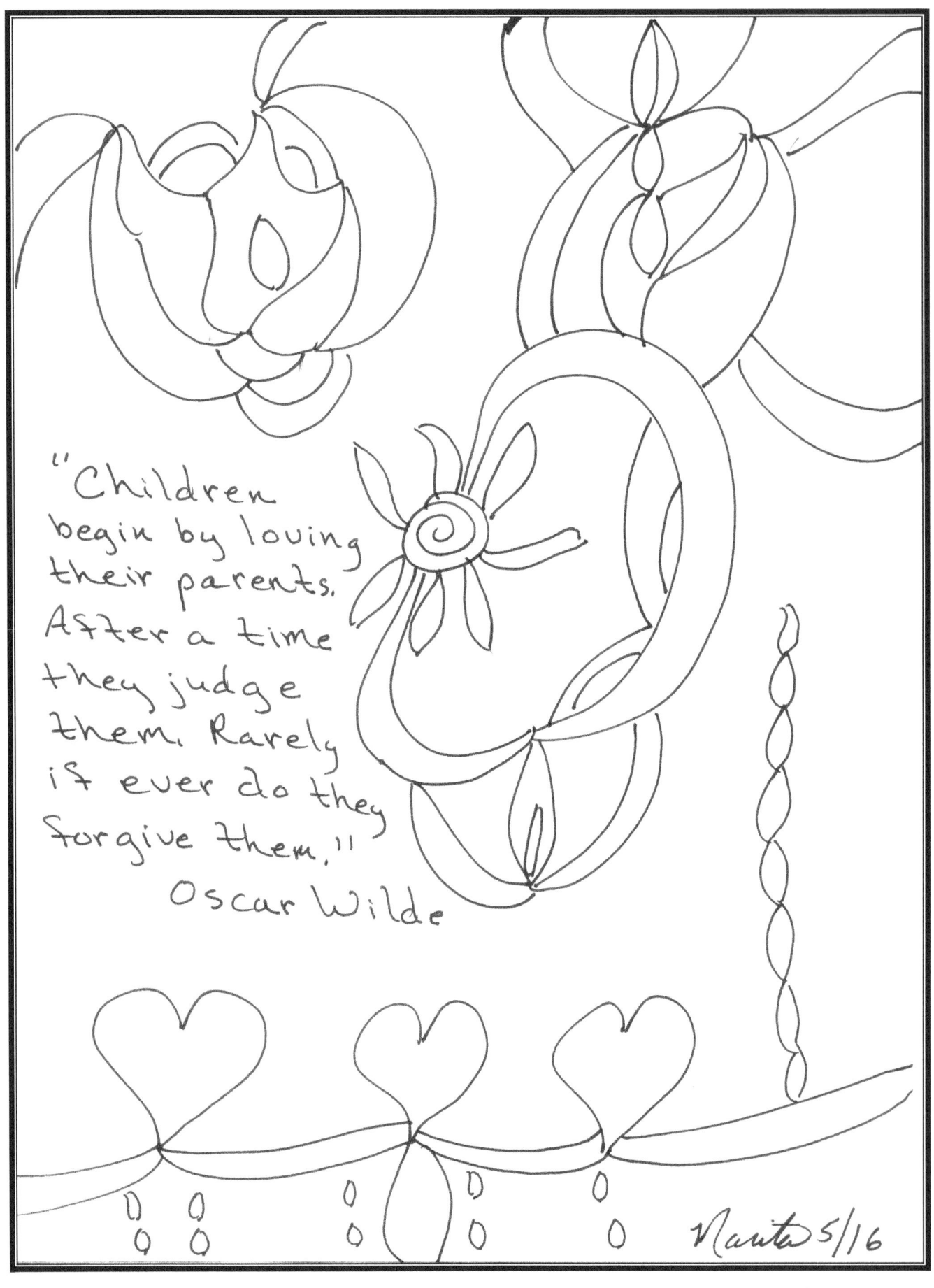

"Children begin by loving their parents. After a time they judge them. Rarely if ever do they forgive them."

Oscar Wilde

Marta 5/16

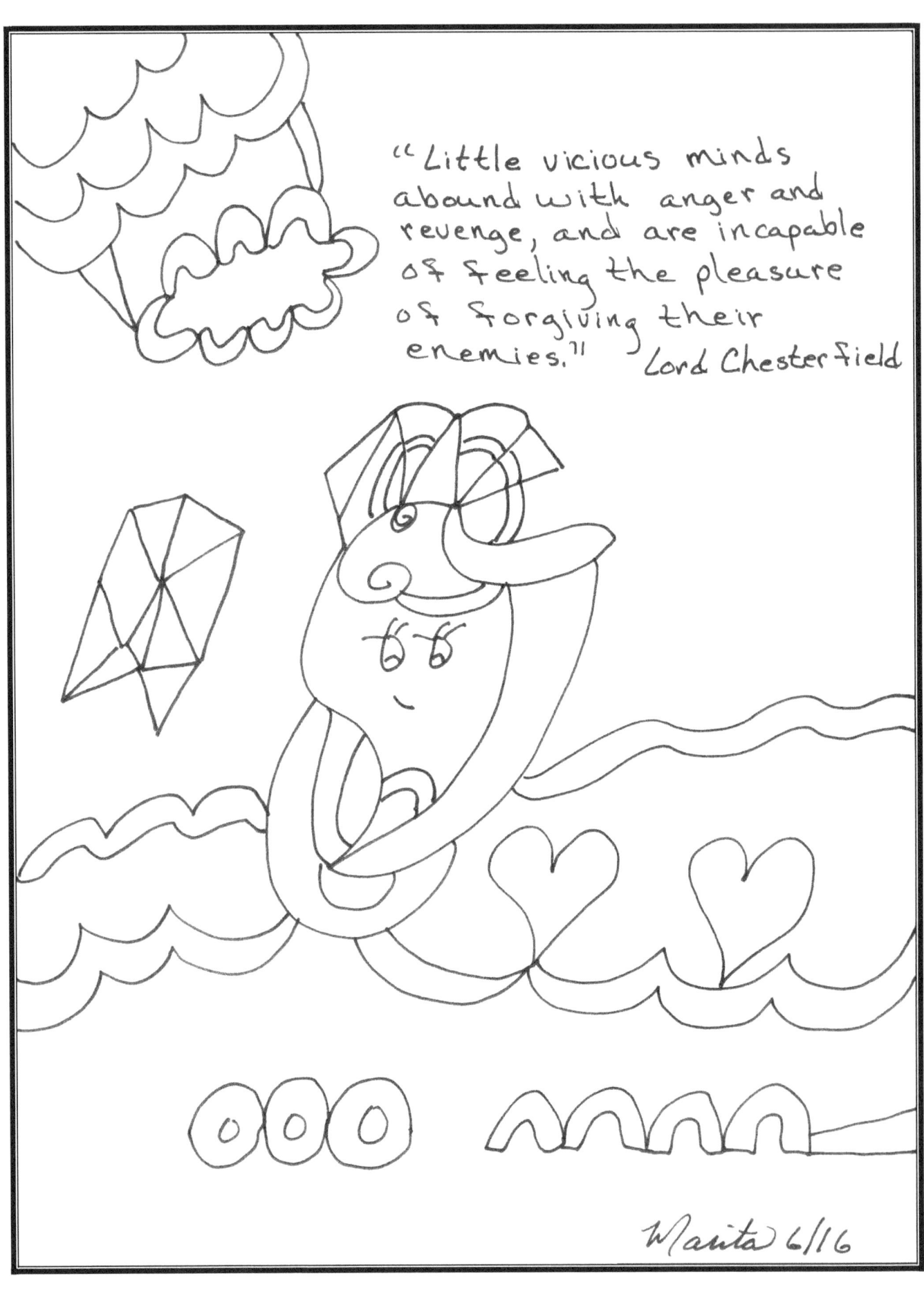

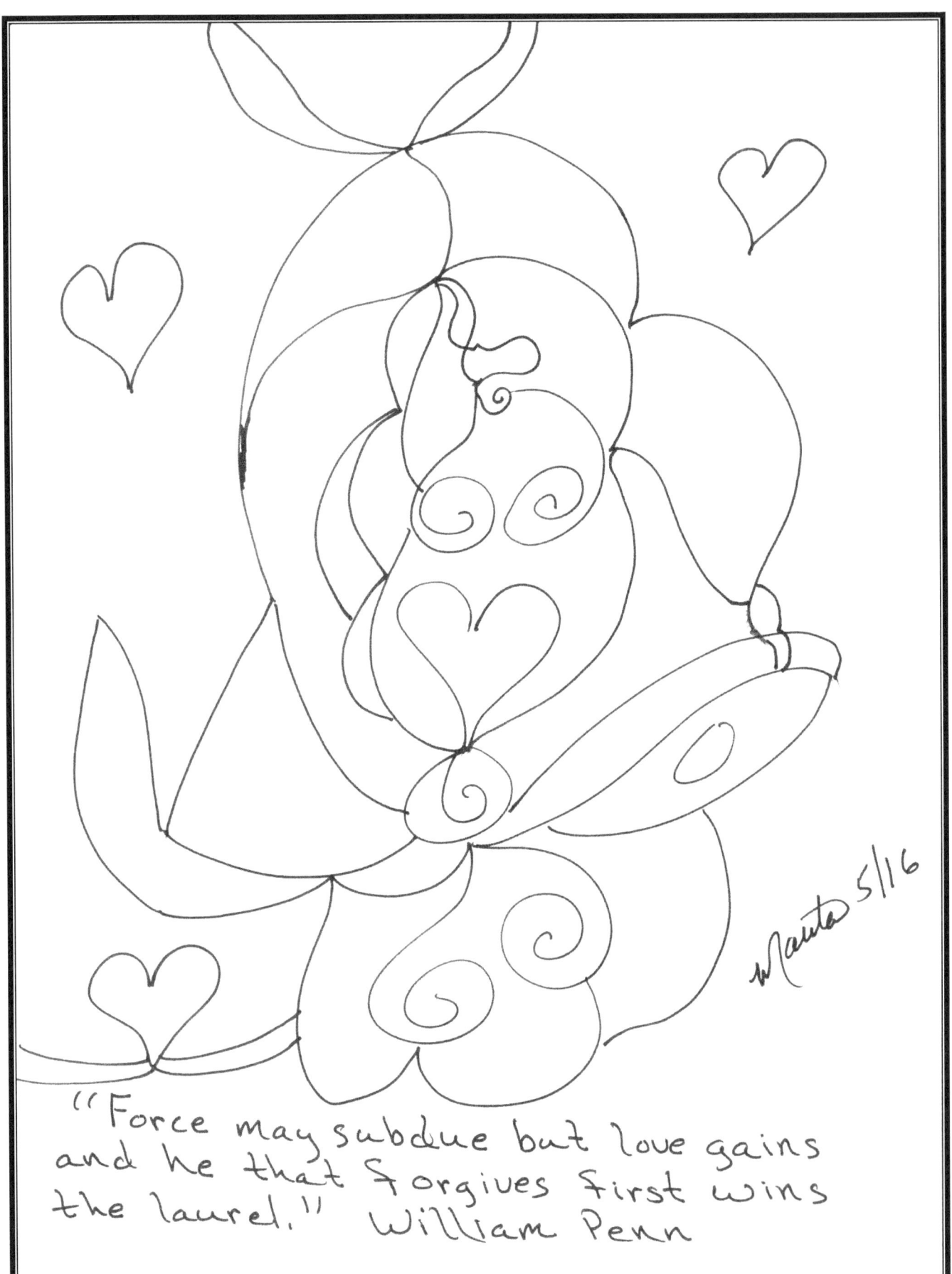

Marta 5/16

"Force may subdue but love gains and he that forgives first wins the laurel." William Penn

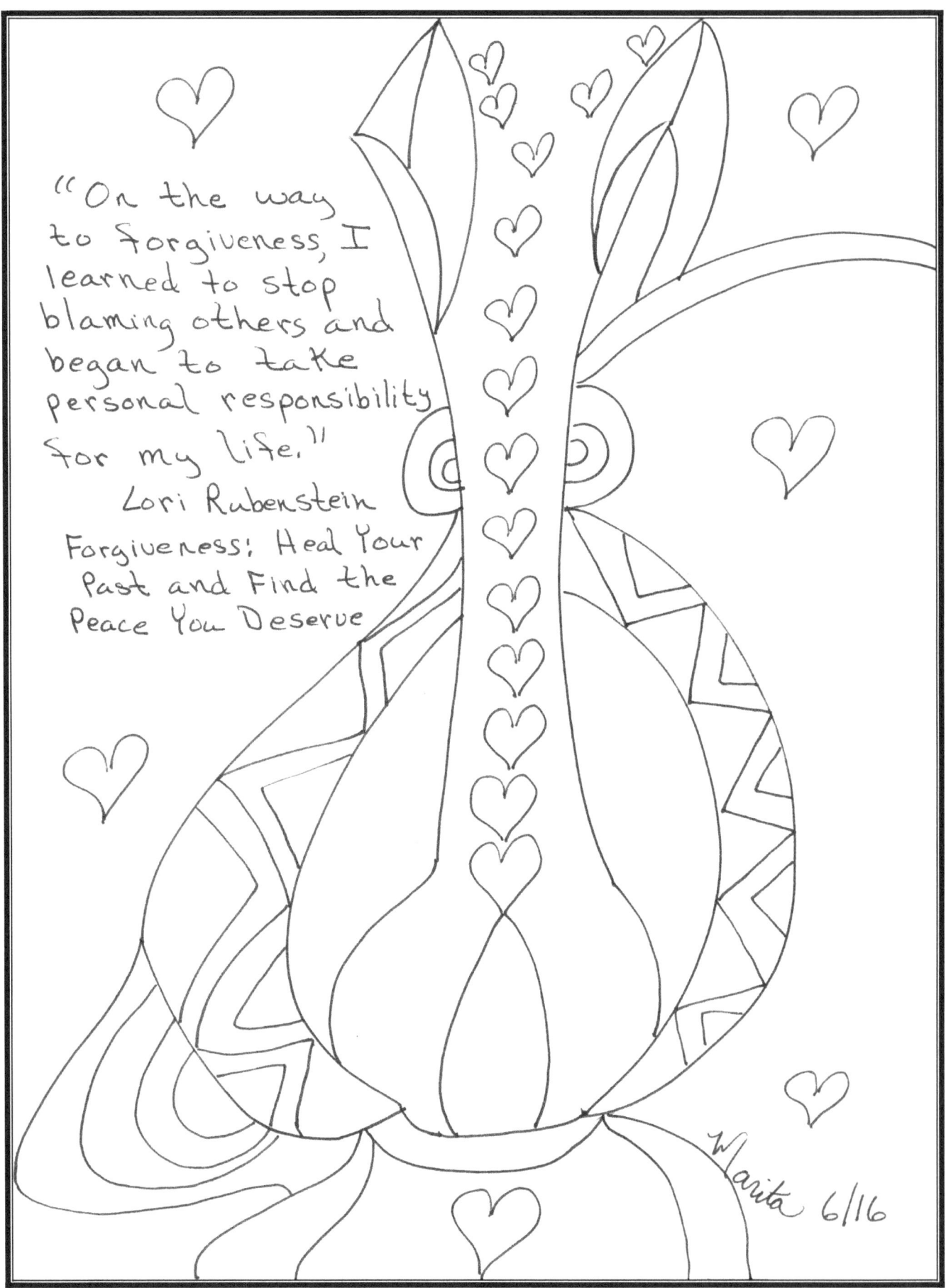

"On the way to forgiveness, I learned to stop blaming others and began to take personal responsibility for my life."
Lori Rubenstein
Forgiveness: Heal Your Past and Find the Peace You Deserve

Marita 6/16

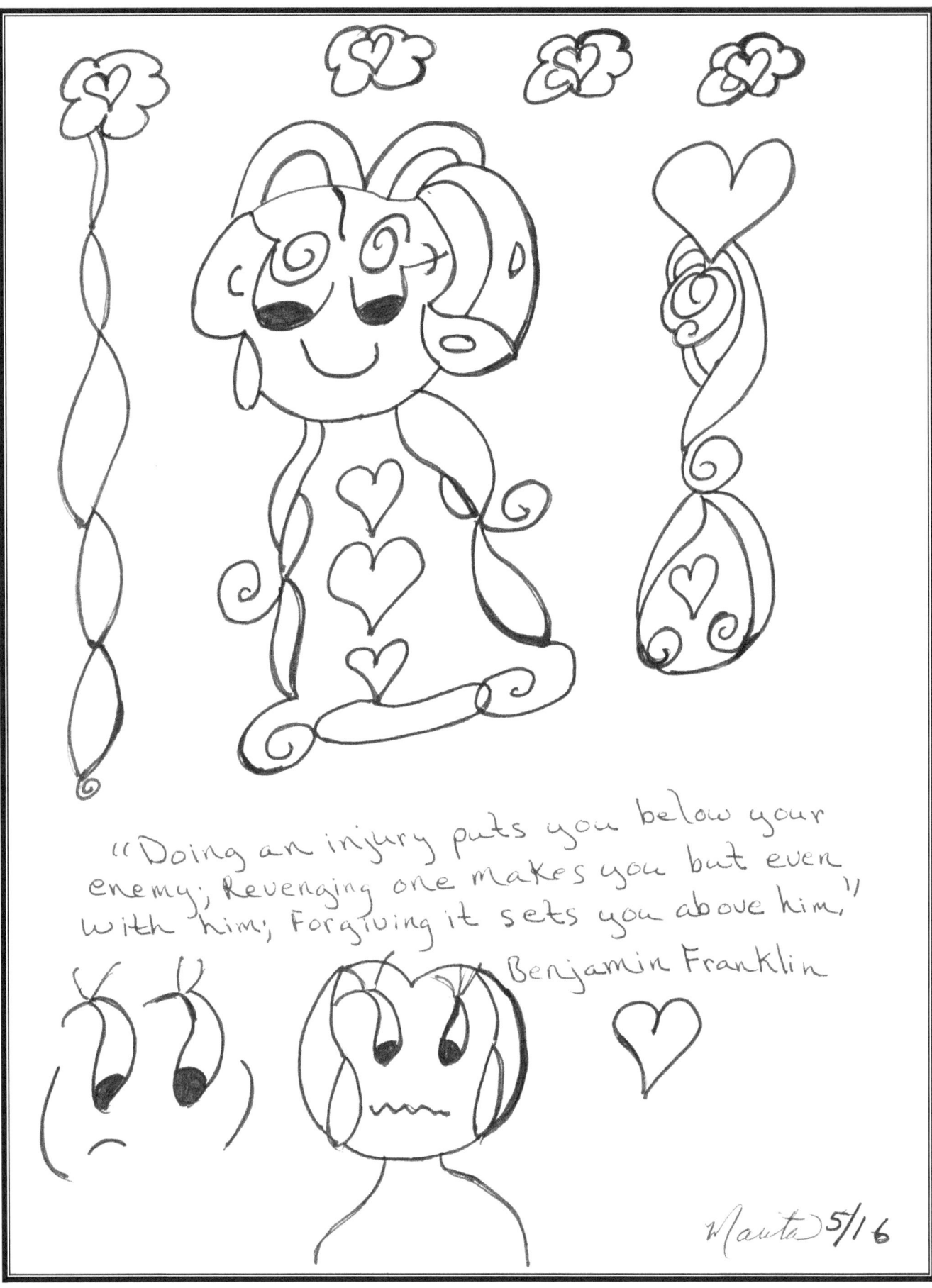

"Doing an injury puts you below your enemy; Revenging one makes you but even with him; Forgiving it sets you above him,"

Benjamin Franklin

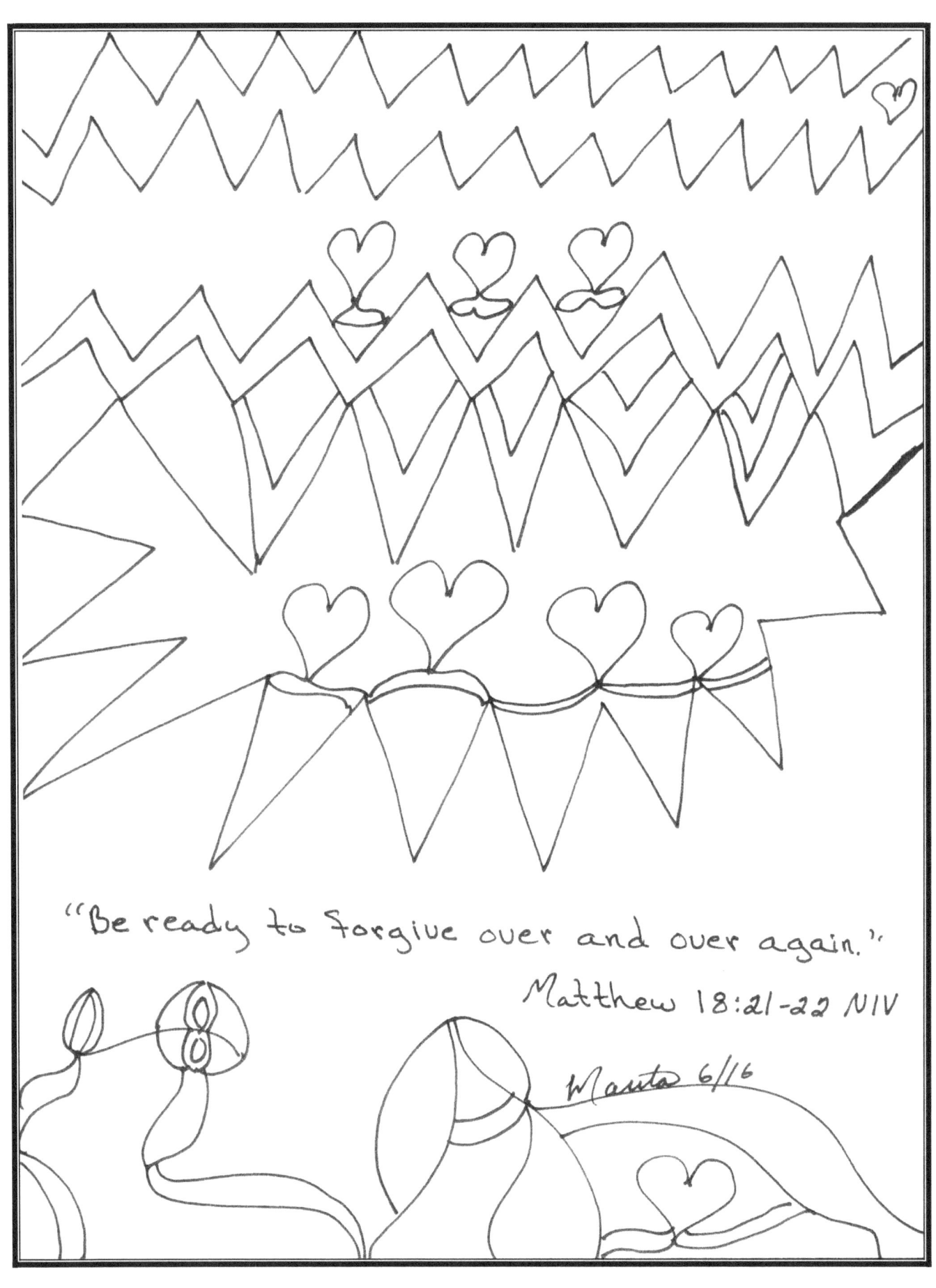

"Be ready to forgive over and over again."

Matthew 18:21-22 NIV

Marta 6/16

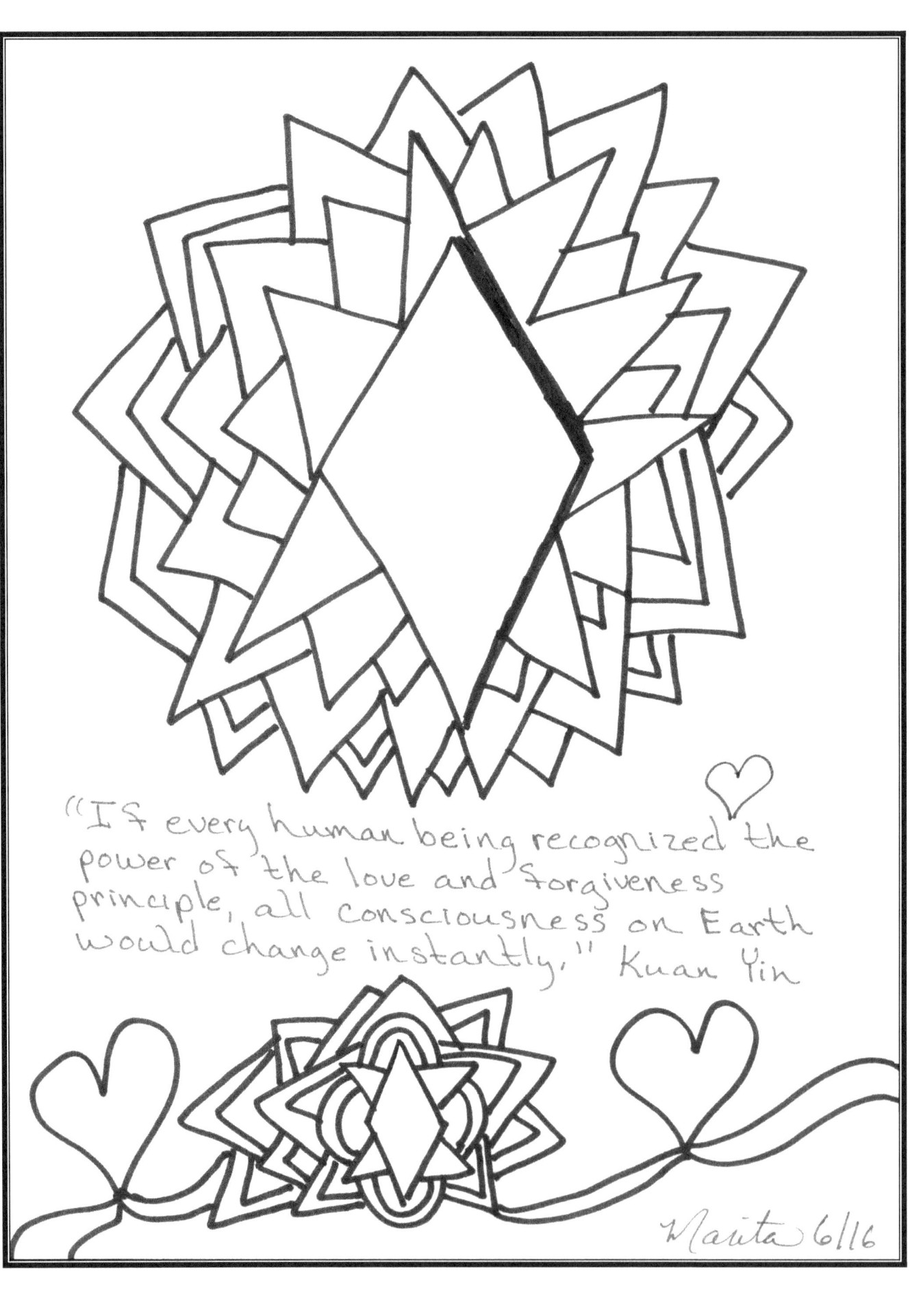

"If every human being recognized the power of the love and forgiveness principle, all consciousness on Earth would change instantly." Kuan Yin

Marita 6/16

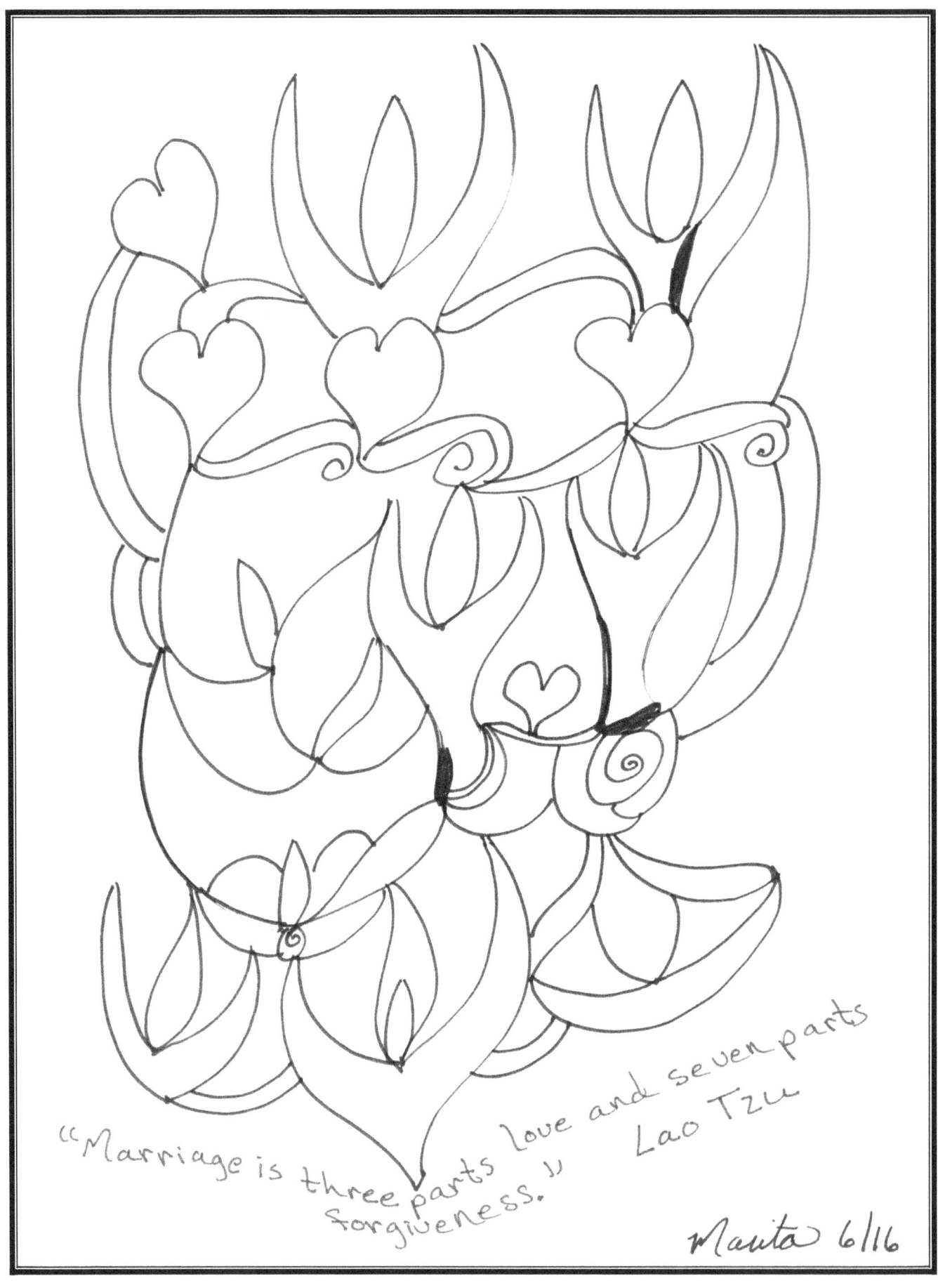

"Marriage is three parts love and seven parts forgiveness." — Lao Tzu

Manta 6/16

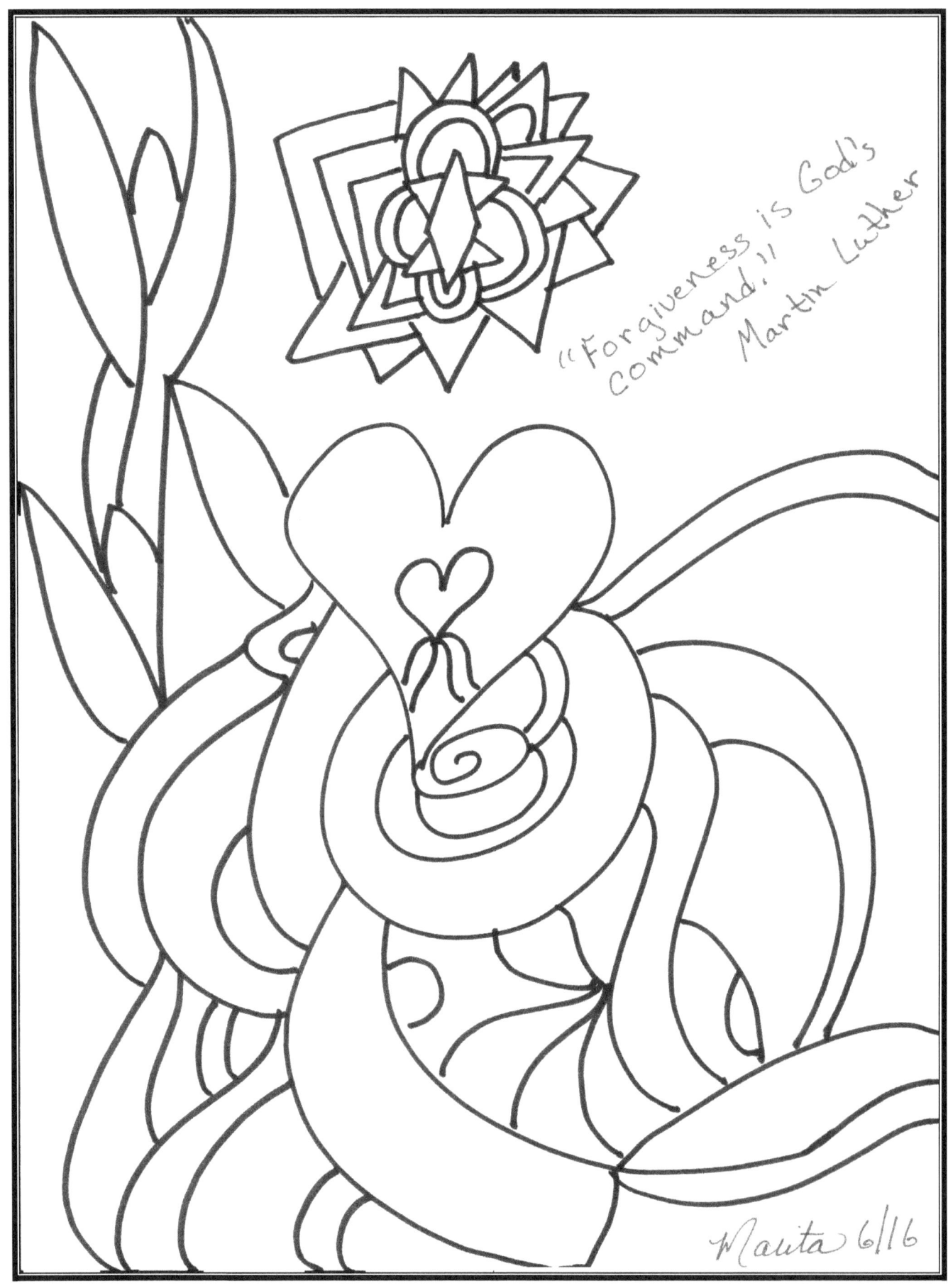

"Forgiveness is God's command!" Martin Luther

Marita 6/16

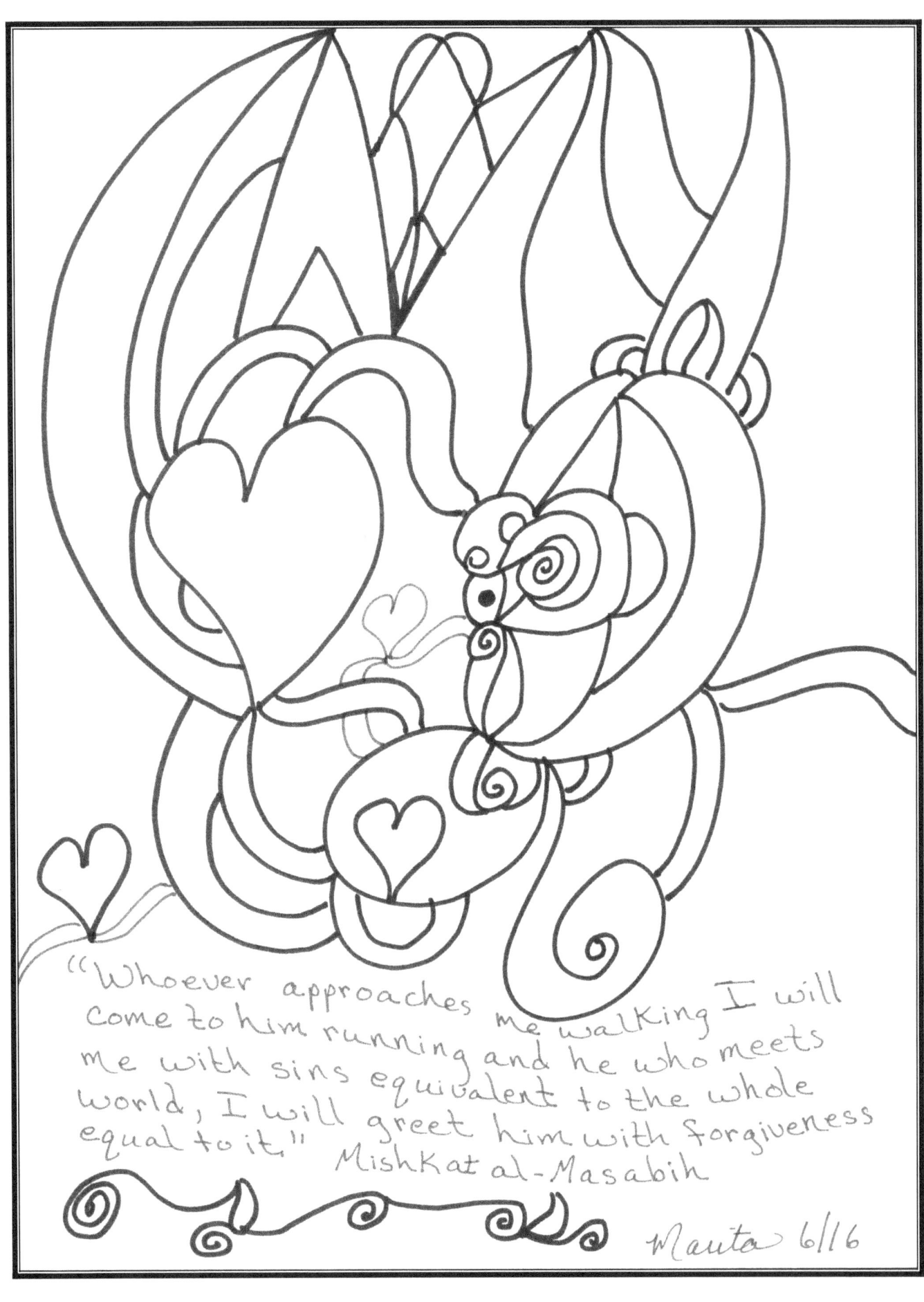

"Whoever approaches me walking I will come to him running and he who meets me with sins equivalent to the whole world, I will greet him with forgiveness equal to it." Mishkat al-Masabih

Maita 6/16

.

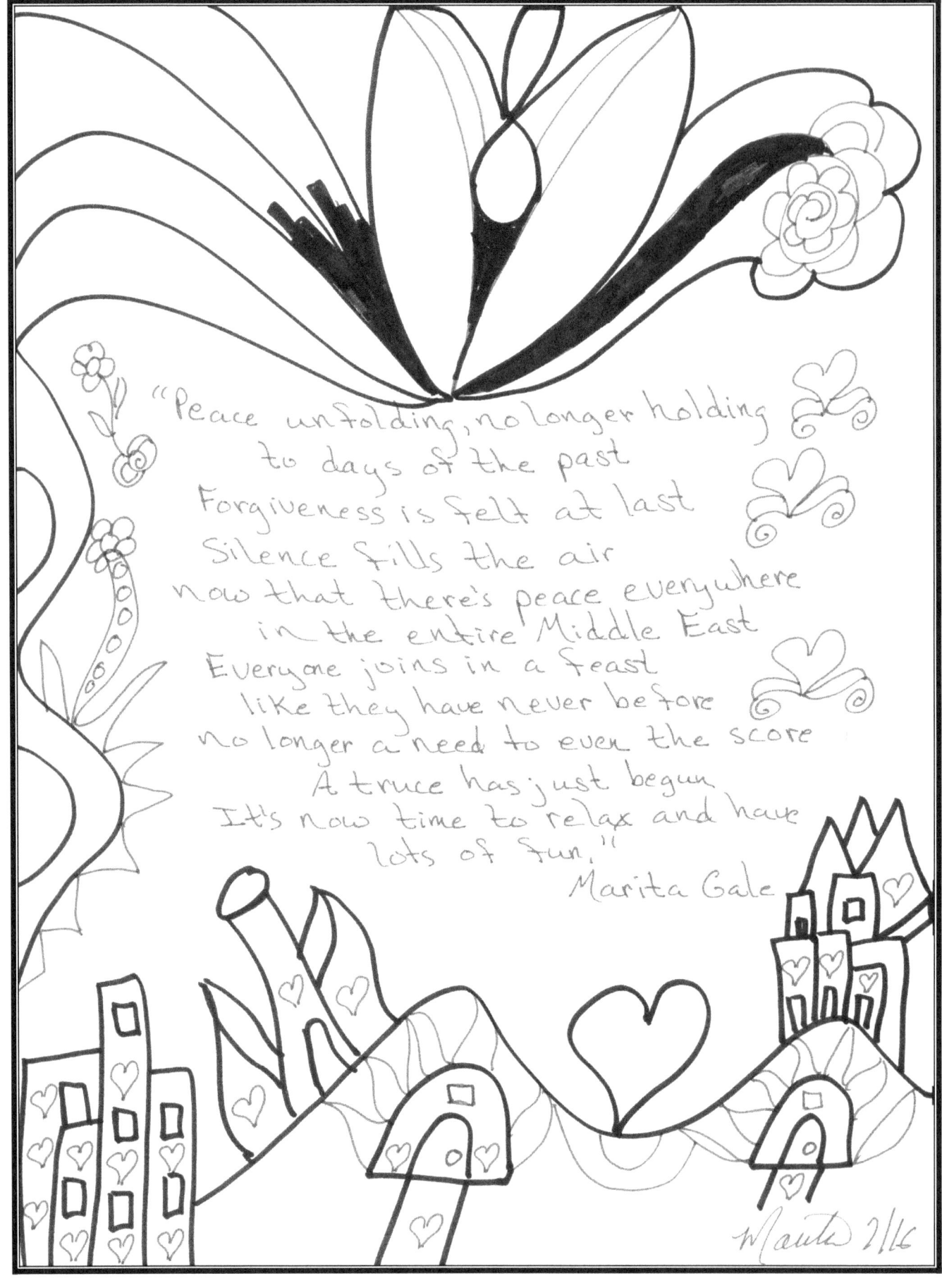

"Peace unfolding, no longer holding
to days of the past
Forgiveness is felt at last
Silence fills the air
now that there's peace everywhere
in the entire Middle East
Everyone joins in a feast
like they have never before
no longer a need to even the score
A truce has just begun
It's now time to relax and have
lots of fun."
                    Marita Gale

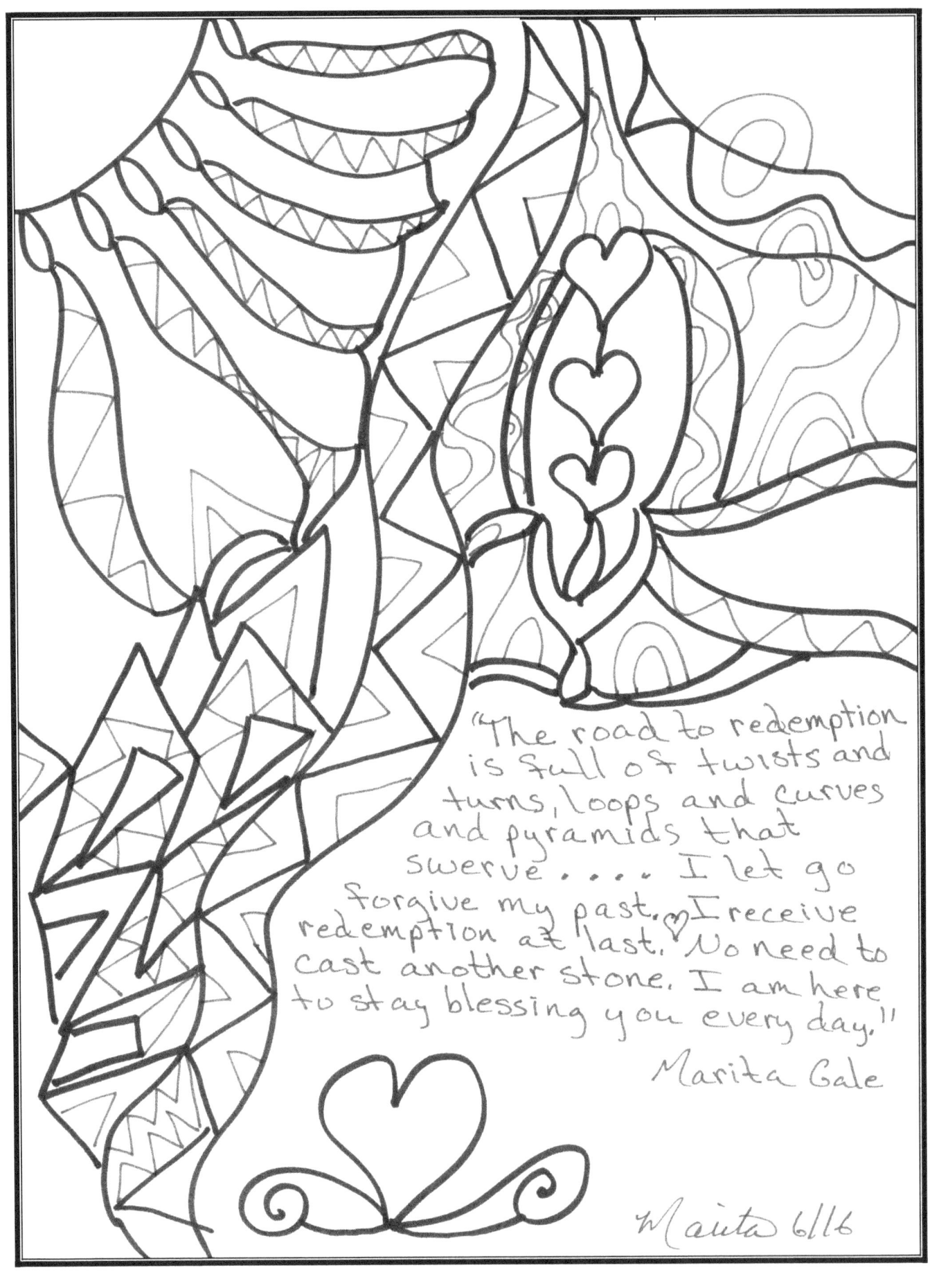

"The road to redemption
is full of twists and
turns, loops and curves
and pyramids that
swerve . . . . I let go
forgive my past. I receive
redemption at last. No need to
cast another stone. I am here
to stay blessing you every day."
                                    Marita Gale

                          Marita 6/16

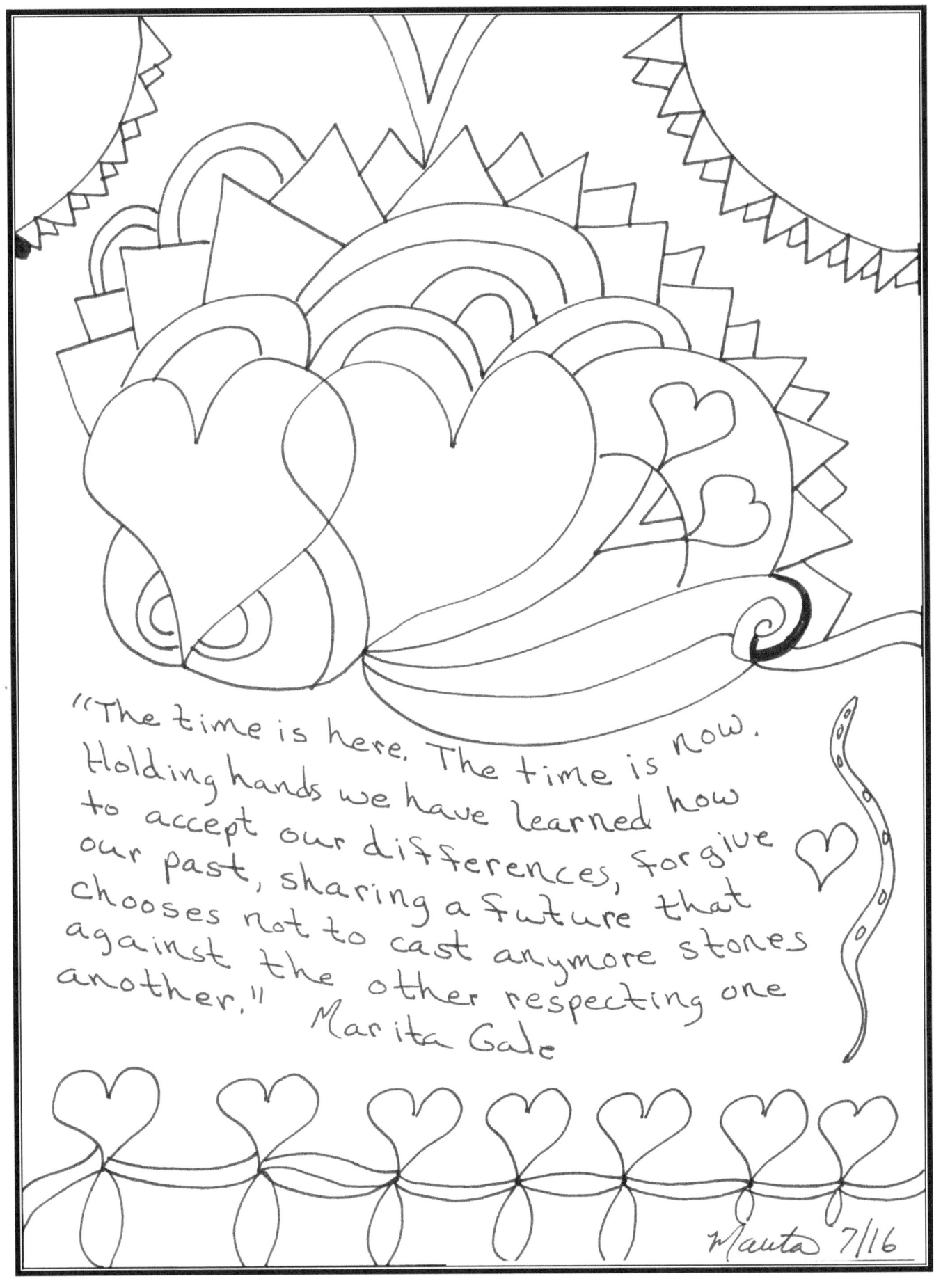

"The time is here. The time is now. Holding hands we have learned how to accept our differences, forgive our past, sharing a future that chooses not to cast anymore stones against the other respecting one another." Marita Gale

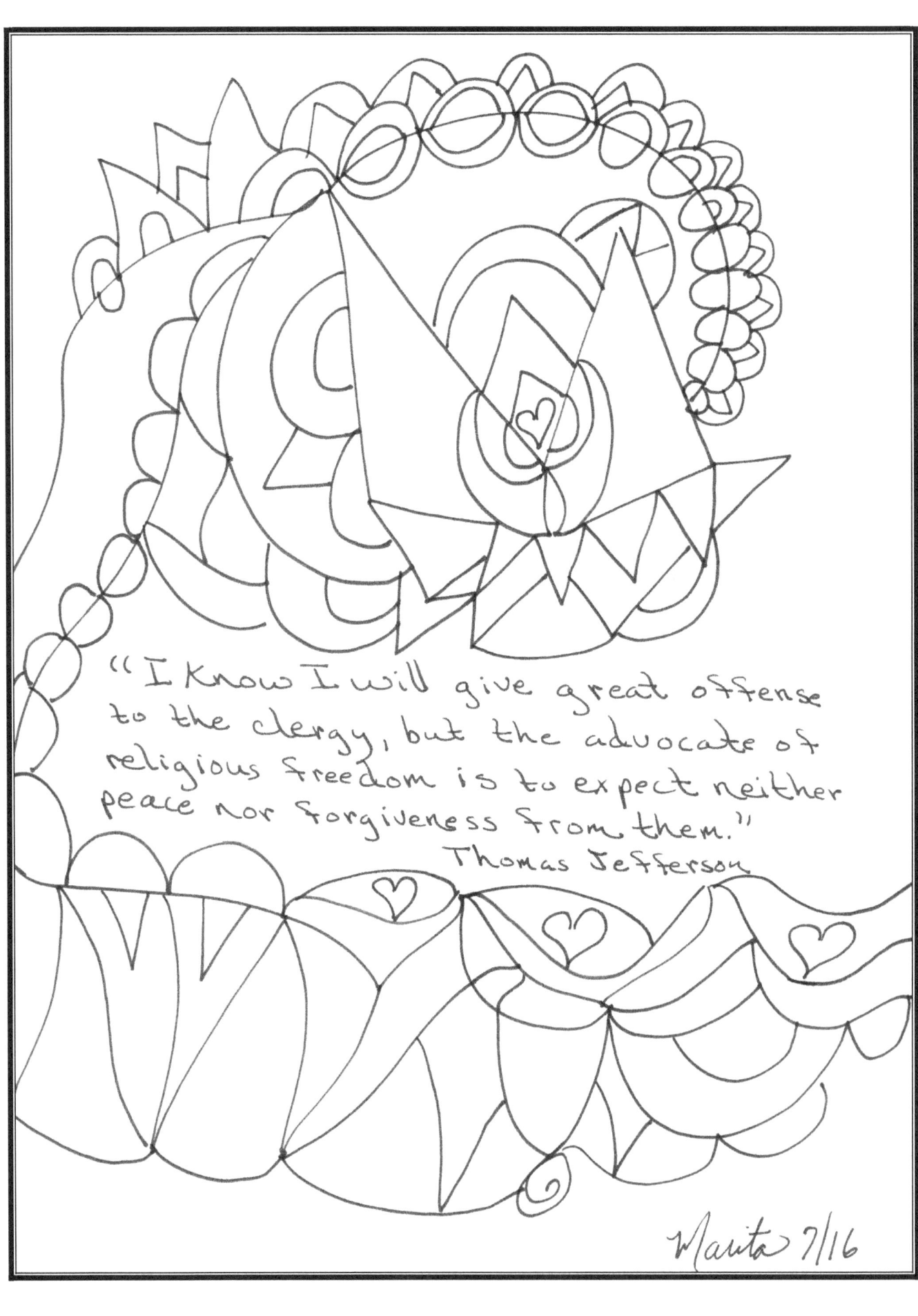

"I know I will give great offense to the clergy, but the advocate of religious freedom is to expect neither peace nor forgiveness from them."
Thomas Jefferson

Marita 7/16

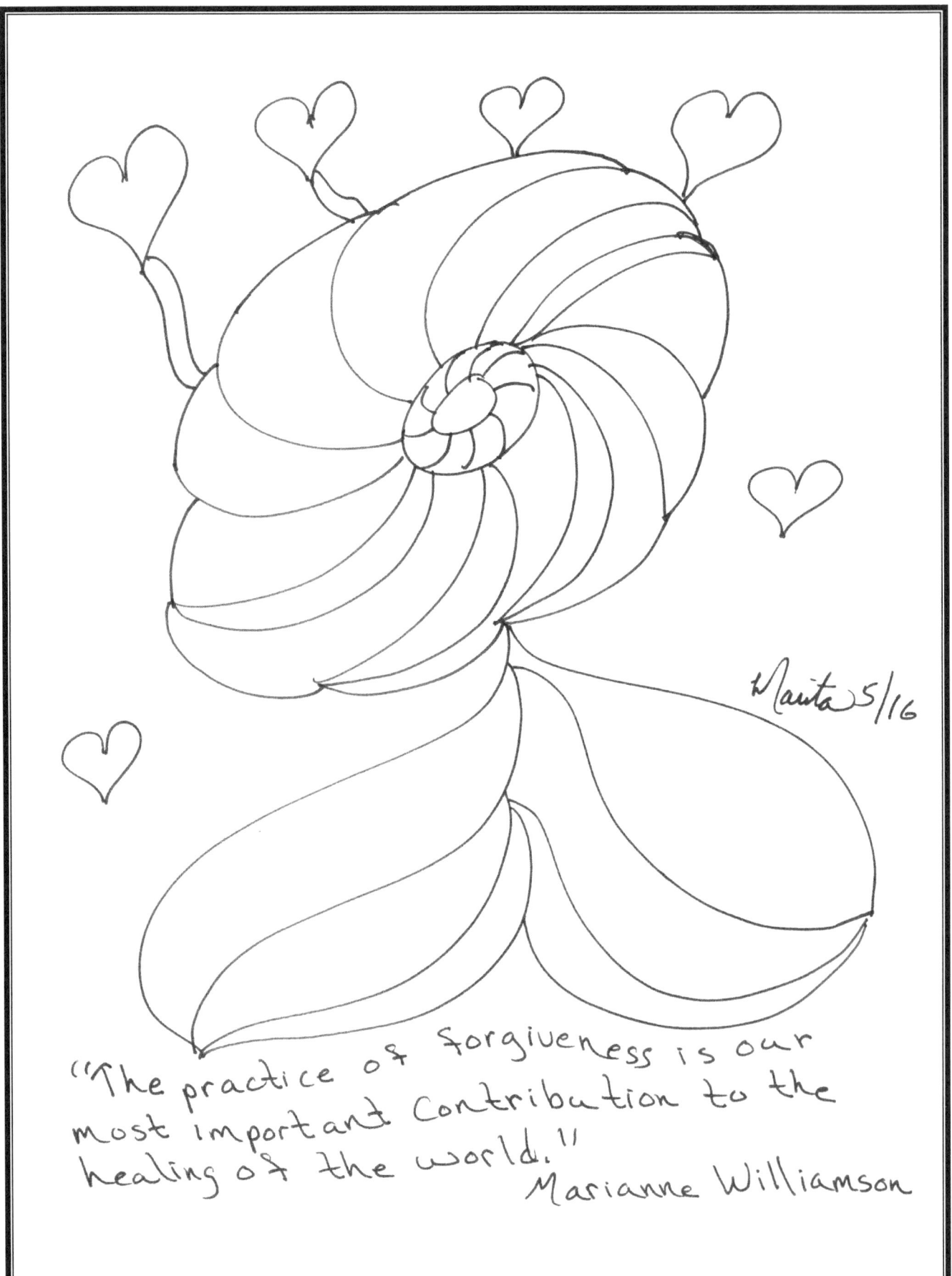

"The practice of forgiveness is our
most important contribution to the
healing of the world."
Marianne Williamson

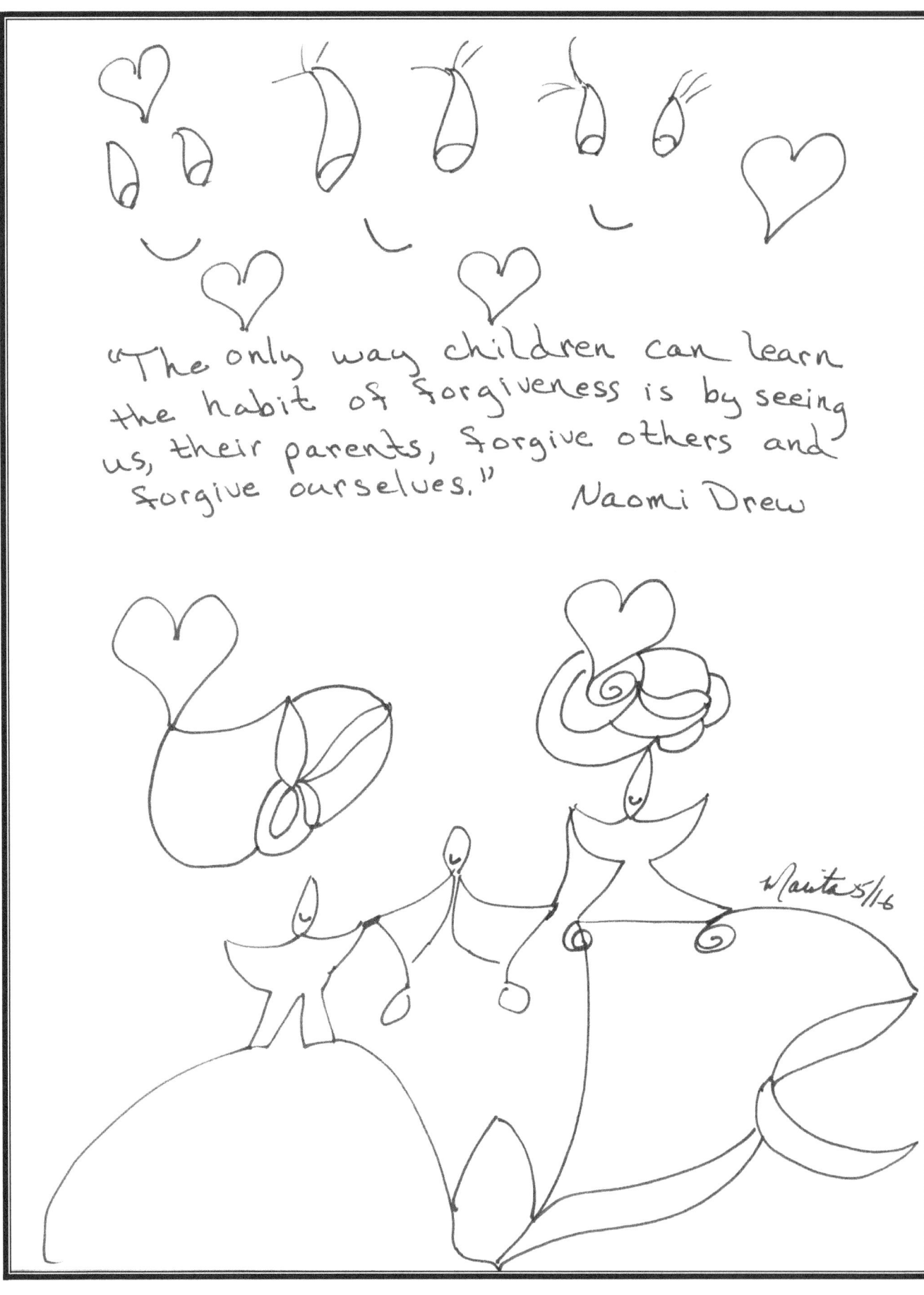

"The only way children can learn the habit of forgiveness is by seeing us, their parents, forgive others and forgive ourselves."

Naomi Drew

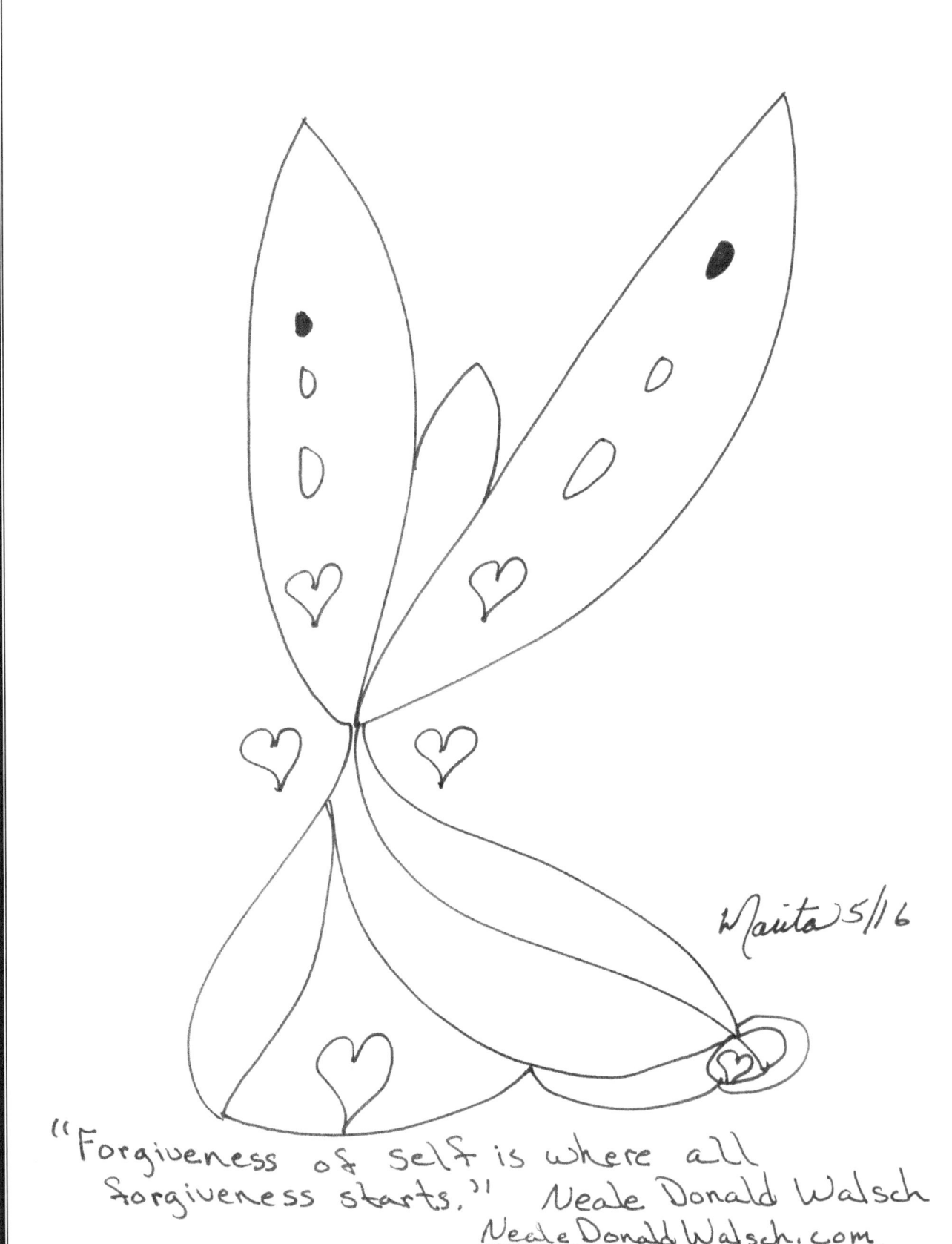

Maita 5/16

"Forgiveness of self is where all forgiveness starts." Neale Donald Walsch

NealeDonaldWalsch.com

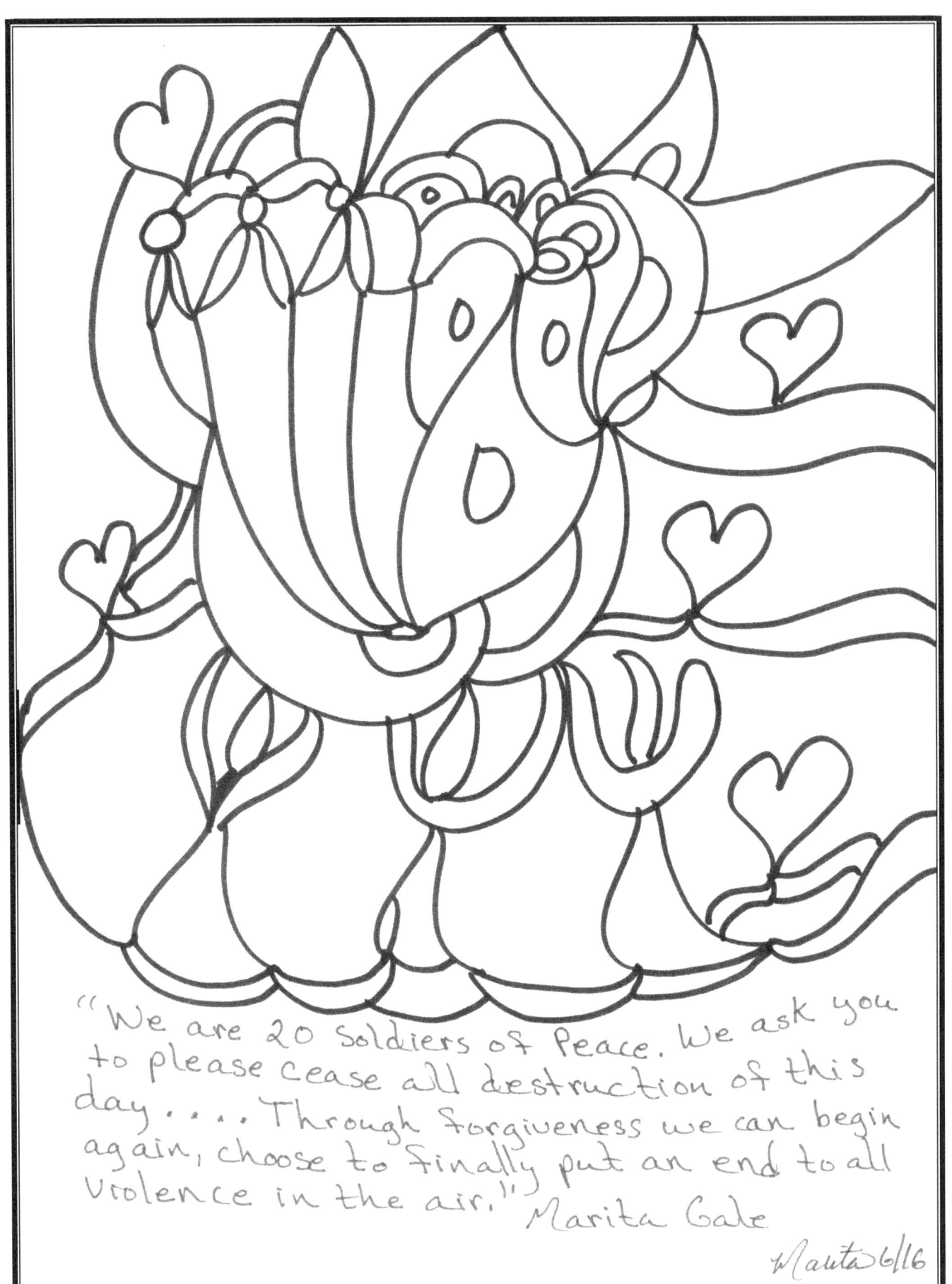

"We are 20 Soldiers of Peace. We ask you to please cease all destruction of this day.... Through forgiveness we can begin again, choose to finally put an end to all violence in the air." Marita Gale

Marita 6/16

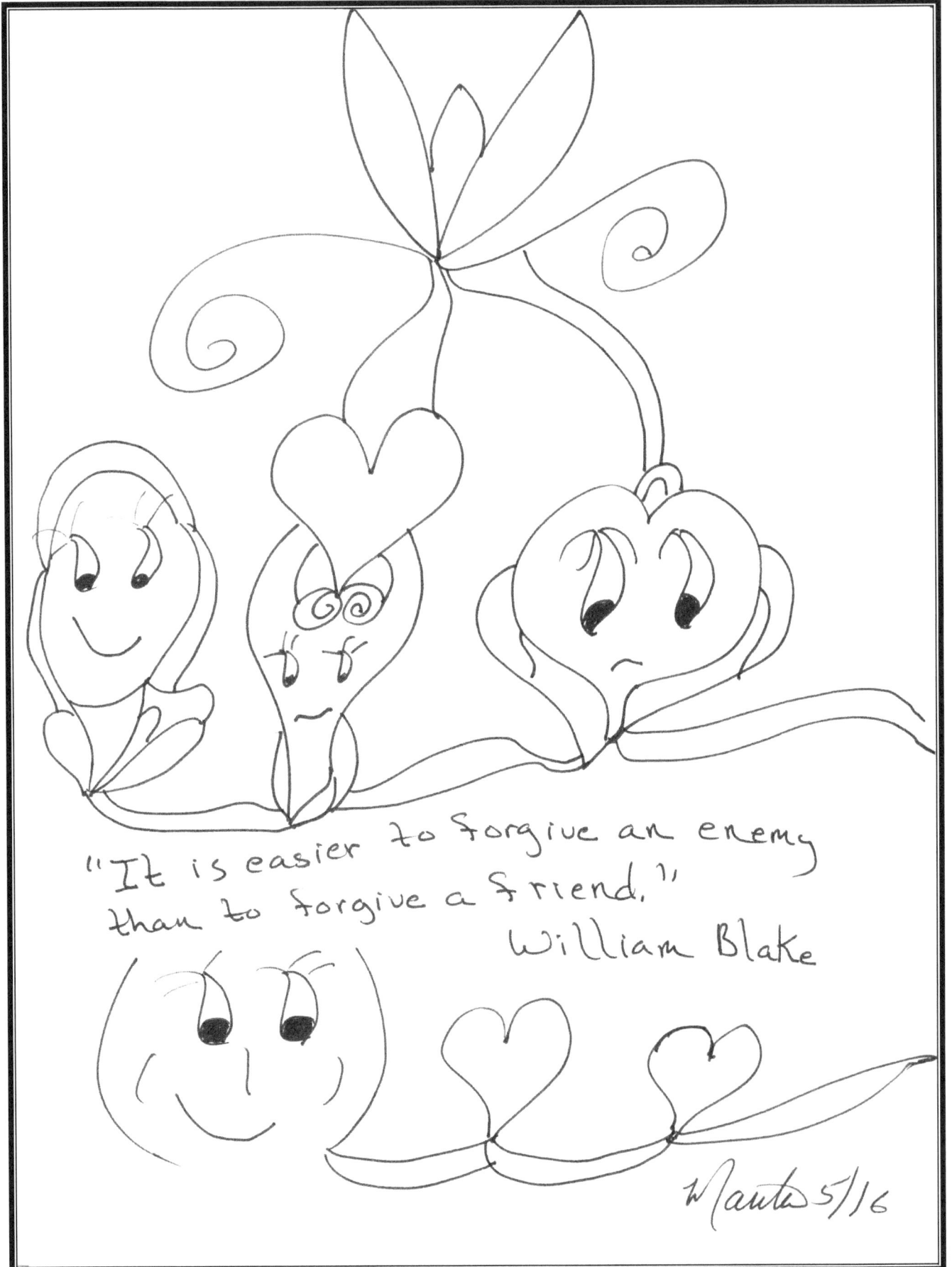

"It is easier to forgive an enemy
than to forgive a friend."
William Blake

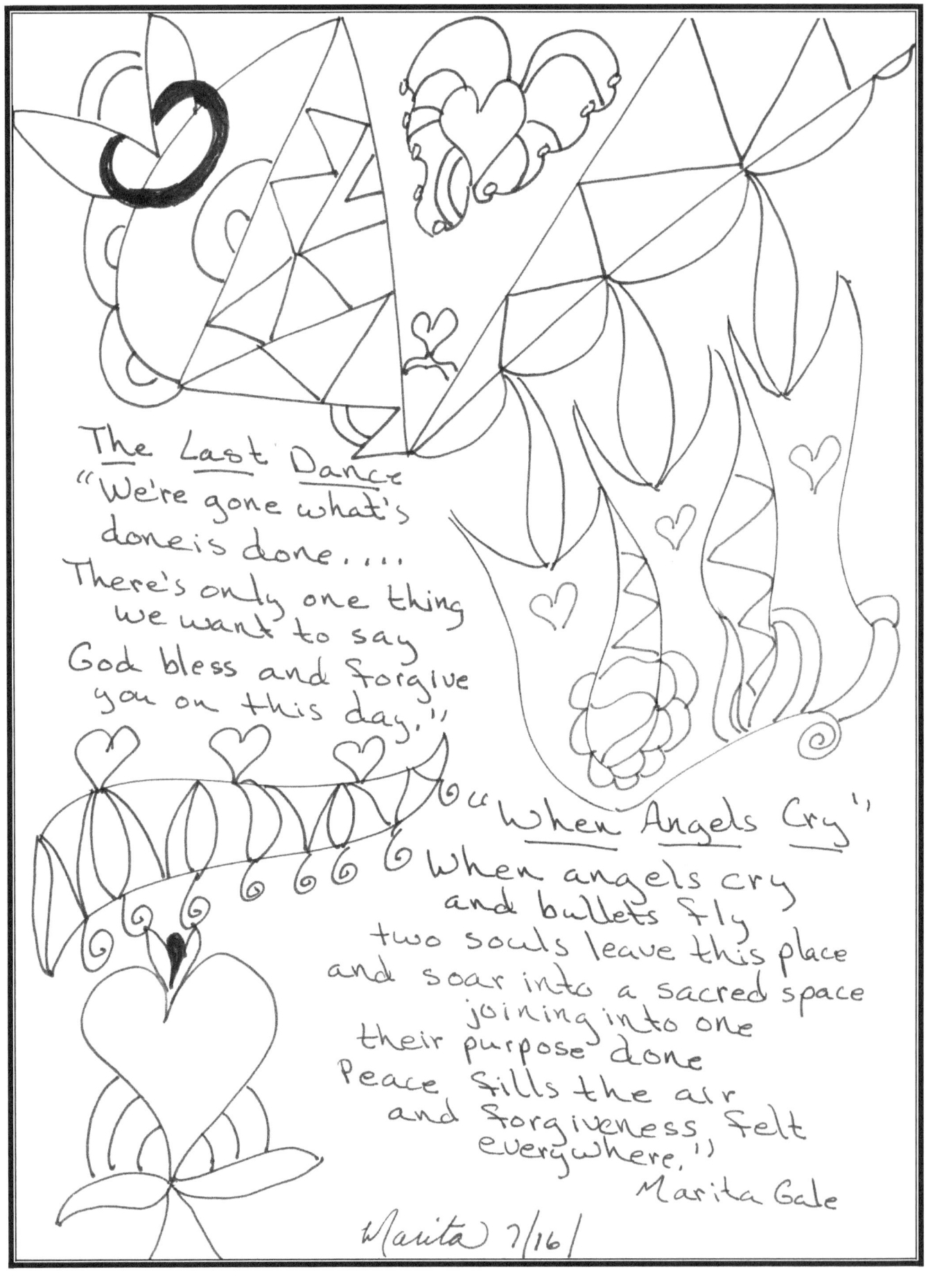

The Last Dance
"We're gone what's
done is done....
There's only one thing
we want to say
God bless and forgive
you on this day,"

"When Angels Cry"

When angels cry
and bullets fly
two souls leave this place
and soar into a sacred space
joining into one
their purpose done
Peace fills the air
and forgiveness felt
everywhere,"
Marita Gale

Marita 7/16/

"God is the Love in which I forgive.
God does not forgive because he has
never condemned, ... those who have accepted
their innocence see nothing to forgive...."

A Course in
Miracles
Lesson 60 (46)

There is nothing to forgive.

Marita 7/16

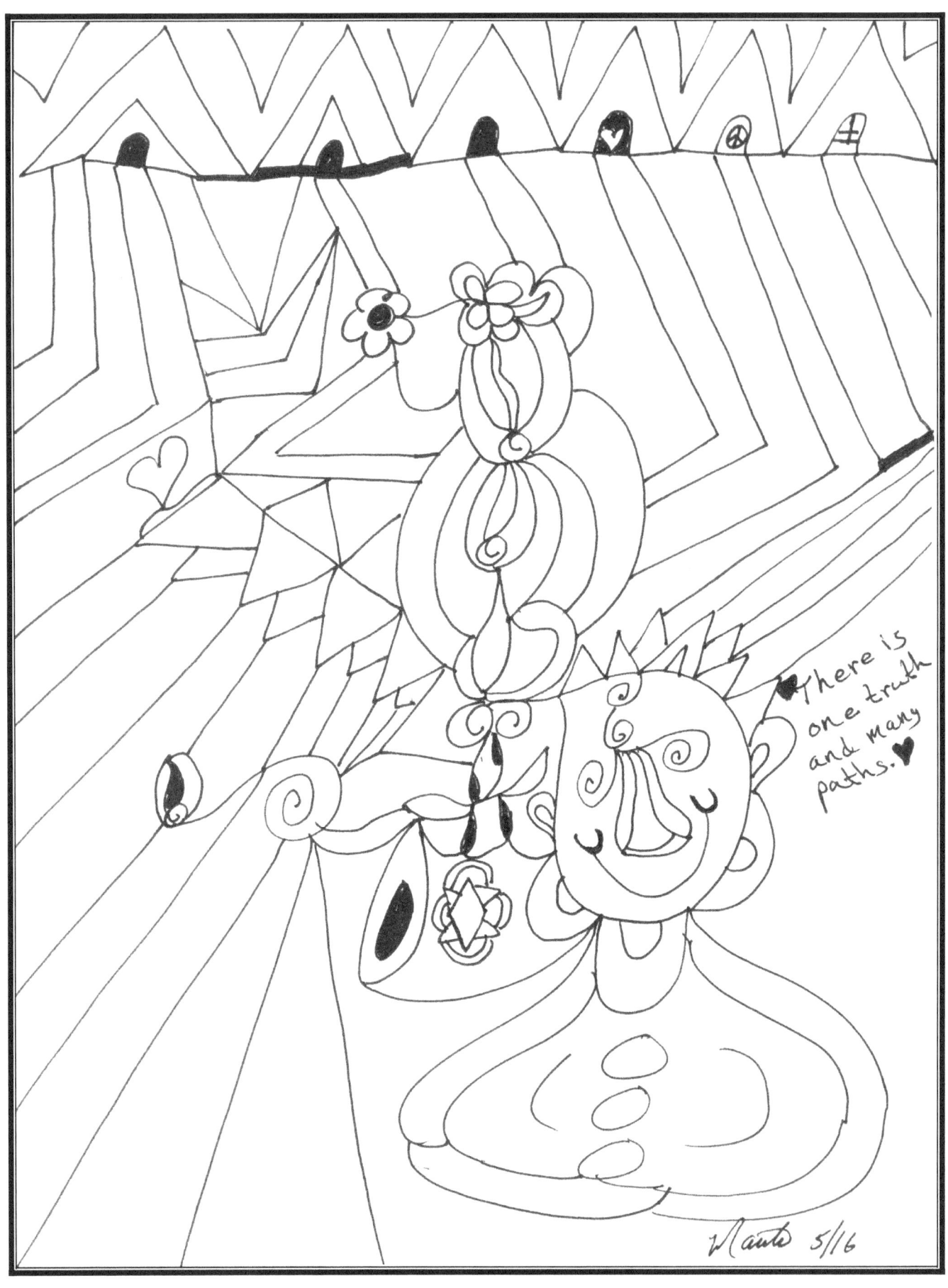

ABOUT THE AUTHOR/ARTIST

Marita's journey began in Knoxville, Tennessee, utilizing her art and poetry as an avenue to find forgiveness allowing personal growth and self-awareness to blossom.

In 2009, Marita loaded all of her personal possessions into her Honda Civic and headed for Sedona, Arizona, trusting her inner guidance to follow her creative path while being of service to others teaching forgiveness through art.

She has created countless energy portraits for people from around the world, authored numerous books which include her artwork and has been a guest speaker in cities across the country.

She was commissioned to do an article with artwork for Unity magazine celebrating mothers in the May/June 2015 issue.

She conducts art workshops across the country and is available for speaking engagements to share her story.

For more information regarding art workshops, individual sessions, or speaking engagements please contact Marita Gale at maritagale@gmail.com or wisdomandartfromtheheart.com.